Half-n-Half

ERIC M. SMITH

PAGE PUBLISHING, INC.
Conneaut Lake, PA

First originally published by Page Publishing 2021

ISBN 978-1-6624-4462-3 (pbk)
ISBN 978-1-6624-4463-0 (digital)

Printed in the United States of America

Contents

Acknowledgments

I would like to start with thanking our parents for giving us life! I give all credit to our Heavenly Father for allowing me to complete this book and being in my life in good as well as bad times. God is good! There are so many people that have made an impact throughout my life and helped me that I hope I don't forget anyone!

My sisters for their encouragement with this project. To my grade school teachers who, through insight, tried to help me and my sisters. Mrs. Green, Mrs. Johnson, Mrs. Brown, my eighth grade teacher! My high school teachers, Mrs. Miles, Mr. Deppe, my high school counselor, and a few other educators that I may have forgotten! My children who I truly Love and have inspired me. Eric II (Mikey), Gabrielle Nicole (Gabby), Kyle (KRS1), Erika, Brittani and Taylor. A special shout-out to Dave and the AV Department at the West Branch Library in Kansas City, Kansas. You all never kicked me off the computers. Thanks so much!

To my church family at New Life Church of the Nazarene. To the fellas at ITS. A special thanks to Ira for always keeping me up with being so silly!

Peggy Bass and her daughters for typing my first *rough* draft, and I do mean rough!

To Pastor Jefferson Newton, my business partner and spiritual advisor. Thanks so much. Barry Anthony contributed in far more ways than he knows. A special thanks to Carmen Newman for just being there. I won't forget it! Randall Wallace and family, you know you owe me a court date! I still got a few skills! The Fields family still eatin' those pot pies! Wayne Benton, much love and admiration! My shirts are starched now.

I apologize if I have not mentioned certain people, but this list could go on forever because of the helpful and encouraging comments from so many people. I hope there is someone out there who will be able to pull something useful from this book! May you receive blessings from God and enjoy a peaceful, healthy, and prosperous life!

Introduction

This book tells how it was growing up biracial! My family survived in Cabrini-Green housing developments (the projects) and the South Side of Chicago. My mother was a German American, and my father was an African American. This is a story that has taken years to put together with the hopes of giving what I like to refer to as an insider's view of one our nation's biggest and seemingly most important issues—the *White and Black* struggle. Our family's story started after our parents met during World War II. They returned home to the United States, and it was a whole different world for our mother, who hadn't ever lived anywhere other than her country, Germany. The time was the early fifties and happened to be when the civil rights movement had begun. My oldest sister, Anita, was the only child born in Germany. The other seven were born here in the United States.

My father opted not to take the Vietnam assignment. I guess he figured he survived WW II and the Korean conflict, and chances were, he wouldn't make it back if he participated in yet another conflict (*war*), so he exited the Army and decided to move back to Chicago, Illinois, the city he and his family moved to early in his life from Mississippi. Chicago probably represented, at the time, a familiar place, as well as a better economic opportunity for him, which meant a better standard of living for his family. History proves Chicago played a very important role in the civil rights movement. Interracial marriages, especially a White-Black one, wasn't accepted anywhere in this country and definitely not within a struggling predominantly Black urban community like Chicago's South Side.

Some countries throughout the world have religious struggles that plague their society, and other countries have severe economic struggles. Our great nation unfortunately still has a mountainous task of getting past a person's skin color. I wrote this book to give anyone interested an honest account of what things were like for me and my particular family.

Does the color of a man's skin still matter in 2002? How does society view interracial marriages today? Some folks would have you believe that the interracial marriage thing is so accepted in modern times, but I can assure you prejudice is very much alive and kicking. My sisters and I were raised in the inner city of Chicago, not some suburb or rural area. I recall thinking that moving to a less congested and not so urban place as Leavenworth, Kansas, we would be better accepted as being biracial. I realized shortly after we moved that we seemed to stand out even in a much smaller city.

I am very comfortable with who I am, but truthfully speaking, it has taken me well into my adult life to reach this comfort zone. I truly hope that this book may give some young person some direction and aid them in attaining a positive identity much earlier in life than it has taken myself and my sisters. I tried hard to write this story with a humorous slant because I recall humor being what made some events bearable.

I have been privileged to inside information from both nationalities. There are very distinct differences in American Whites and American Blacks. We should work toward understanding and dealing with those differences better. My one hope is that the information in this book can help a biracial or mixed person attain a true sense of identity!

1

A Vicious Start

The Projects

It was cloudy today as I looked up and tried to see our apartment, which was located on the ninth floor. Cabrini-Green projects, I recall thinking, looked extremely tall to a young child. I have read a variety of writings from several psychologists about how far back a child's memory actually starts and how much detail can be replayed. There are many conclusions about memory recollection from noted intellectuals. They seem to have agreed on one fact—a traumatic situation or single event could cause a child's memory to recall an event or a certain situation very early. Whatever their conclusions, I know without a shadow of a doubt that throughout my life, I had been able to recall very vividly living in those projects. I was about five when I was actually able to take notice of things that happened around our way. Of course, I wasn't aware for some years later that we lived in one of the nation's most dangerous housing projects.

The mornings were the quietest and least dangerous part of the day. After my older sisters were off to school, I asked my mom if I could go outside to the playground. Even though she was very protective, Mom would let me go downstairs for a short while.

"Eric Michael, you stay in the play area, and I'll call you to come up." Our apartment windows happened to have a view straight downstairs, so Mom felt she could keep an eye on me playing. Now until that day, I never paid attention to the things going on in the stairwells or out front in the courtyard. This day, I have often been able to recount that there were a few people standing around in the hallways and sitting on the benches in the front of our building. Once on the playground, I would look up to see our apartment. There were a few kids on the swings and the sliding board. I couldn't have been out there very long when two boys, possibly a year or two older than me, started calling me names.

"Hey, White boy...why are you playin' down here? You better get off our swing."

I hadn't really had this type of thing happen that I could recall, so I remember just looking at them, feeling like I was frozen.

"These are not your swings... I live here too." No sooner had I said that than they both bum-rushed me and threw a couple of punches and kicks. I wasn't a fighter at that young age, but I knew I was pretty fast even back then. I flew out of the play area and didn't stop running until I reached our apartment. I burst through the door. I must have startled my mom. She grabbed me and saw that I was almost out of breath.

"Eric, what in the world is wrong?" I was breathing so hard I didn't think I was able to speak. Once Mom let me catch my breath, she again asked in her very familiar German accent, "Son, what is wrong?"

"Mom, I was playing, and two boys started calling me names and then tried to beat me up." I recall looking intently into my mom's beautiful eyes. Our mom was a true fighter. I don't mean physically. She was a very tough young German woman.

"Eric, are these two boys much bigger than you?"

"No, Mom. They are my size." Why did I say that? All I wanted to do was have my mom hug and kiss me and tell me to stay inside and bring me something she had baked! Man, Mom was always cooking and baking something.

"Eric Michael, you get back down those stairs, and you better learn right now not to let people push you around."

I thought, *I am scared to death.* I recall maybe fighting and getting beat up by my sisters, but they would also fix me a snack or watch television with me after they knocked me around. I was often asked when I was older and people saw how I defended myself or how well I could box if the area I grew up in made me so tough.

I told people, "Naw, it was my sisters beaten me up." I grabbed this miniature bat someone had given me and ran back downstairs, not sure what I was going to do, but I did think of the bat as an equalizer since there were two of them and my backups (sisters) were at school. I put the bat up my sleeve. I remember thinking that I didn't want to use that bat to hit someone. Mom always said, "If you don't have to fight, don't!"

The two boys were playing and acted like nothing happened when they saw me enter the playground. "What did I do that y'all started calling me names and punching on me?"

"White boy, you don't have to do nothin'. My daddy don't like White people, so I don't like White people."

"Well, my mom says y'all ain't makin' me leave. I can play here."

Again, the two boys started walking toward me with their fists balled up and with real tough looks on their faces. I pulled the little bat out and started chasing them through the play area and all the way to another building before I stopped.

When I look at my youngest son, Kyle, and see how he runs everywhere he goes, he often reminds me of events I had at an early age. We race from time to time, and he asks me if he is faster than me when I was his age. I tell him I think he is faster than I was. I also relate to him that a lot of the time, I had to run out of necessity rather than around a track as he does. He just laughs and makes his typical face. As I walked back to our building, I kept replaying what had happened. I thought, what would make these boys pick me out of the other kids playing, and why did they keep calling me a White boy? I ran upstairs, and since we lived on the ninth floor, the run upstairs alone was a workout.

Once upstairs, I asked my mom what those boys meant when they called me a White boy. My mom carried an enormous burden of raising us at home because my father worked two jobs. "Eric, they don't know what they're talking about. They probably are saying what their parents say at home." Our parents never really addressed us being biracial, and since I am older now and have had the opportunity to look at this issue from a grown person's perspective, I realize that parents definitely should talk to their children and instill in them an identity from both nationalities and cultures. This event and others like it, at such an early age, made me the young man I was. That single event made me turn into an aggressor in my teens and young adult life. I often had situations come up with dudes either trying to rob me or simply make me back down. I would think of that event and flip the script on them. I would rob them or would do whatever it took to make them back up.

I am forty-two, and I have children of my own. I know my father worked day and night to get us out of those projects. Maybe if there were talk shows back then or if we lived in a more rural area, we all would not have the memories of tough childhoods that seemed to center around the fact that we were born from a Black father and White mother. People need to realize that the things they expose their children to at an early age are often what molds their children's thoughts and behavior.

I recall having to walk down the stairs because the elevators represented an unknown danger if we were without our father, who made it very plain that he was strapped and had no problem dealing with whoever tried to bother us. I remember, at the age of fifteen and being a tenth grader at Calumet High School, carrying a .32 revolver, a straight razor, and a pair of brass knuckles everywhere I went. I had younger sisters. If trouble didn't come at me, it often involved the protection of my little sisters. Everywhere we went, even grown folks, White or Black, asked us what we were. I had gotten a pretty nasty attitude about that question. If someone asked that, I often acted like I didn't hear them at first. If they asked it a second time, I would reply, "What do you think I am?" and walk off, not giving a damn what they thought of the answer.

We either saw or were actually involved in family fights. We folk hung out on corners until the wee hours of the morning. We saw shootouts, people bleeding, running up the street hollering, and gangbangers chasing people. People unfortunately lived in very rough areas, but when you are different, you stand out at a time and in situations when your safety is often compromised. I totally agree with the statement that a person or people without an identity no doubt goes through life like a ship with no sail.

I realize times are tough, and often people must choose an area that they can afford to provide a roof for their family. You, too, can encourage and give your children a positive role model and good self-identity. Don't let your children be exposed to such a *vicious start*!

2

The Move

Even though I'm forty-two years old, I can still recall the big move to the South Side. The excitement that was displayed by my family spilled over to me. I remember everyone looked as if we won a current-day lottery. If you, the reader, can only imagine seeing nine people getting off this bus at the corner of Eighty-Second and Halsted and walking one block east to Emerald and seeing our new house. It was a feeling that is, to this day, a magnificent one. If anyone has lived in the projects and then has moved out to a house or even a smaller apartment or duplex, you should remember the sense of being freed. I remember the things my sisters were saying: "I know what room I've got" and "Eric, your room is in the basement." And we actually had a basement and an upstairs with rooms. In addition to that, we had a front and backyard with little patches of grass here and there. Cabrini-Green didn't have very much grass, and you definitely didn't have a yard to say that was your own. The first thing a person would notice was all the quietness that surrounded you, even when arriving in the morning. The "projects" were slow motion most mornings, but I couldn't ever remember my past surroundings being this tranquil at any part of the day or night.

After what seemed to be a complete examination of our new house by all of us, I recall slipping away outside, sitting on the front porch, and thinking if this was going to be our house or if someone would come and tell us we had to move back to that nightmare of a courtyard with concrete instead of grass that seemed so far away from this place, as if you're standing outside and looking up to the sky and seeing the moon. All I could do was pray that this would be our new place to live. My sisters appeared to be very different from the previous day, so relaxed and at ease with themselves and our surroundings. Of course, as a grown man looking back, I know that at this time they didn't feel threatened by this quiet and what seemed to be paradise. Our area was a mixed neighborhood with White families and Black families who, we would find out later, mostly migrated from some other public housing development throughout the city.

After we were assigned different chores, we cleaned up and got things settled. For one of our first times, there were no arguments coming from anyone in the house. I think all my sisters were so glad to be out of those rows of tall buildings that no chore or assignment was too difficult. The look on my mother's and father's faces were different. Mom's had a look of relief, and Pop's had a distinct look of feeling the pride he deserved for rescuing his family from the constant turmoil and what no doubt he would have noticed as possibly a life-threatening situation if we remained.

Our block, Emerald, was also named the dead end because of the brick wall at the end of the street that supported the train tracks overhead. A train would come by at least daily and throw down white chalk to us kids. We would scream at the top of our lungs for the train conductors to toss us some down to the streets. We would use the chalk for four squares. The boys would draw a square on the brick wall to play a game we called strikeout. The girls would use their pieces to draw hopscotch or sit around and write who liked so-and-so.

Looking back, I can remember thinking about those men we saw riding the train. I wondered where they were coming from or where they might be headed and if they were having fun traveling around from city to city, seeing different places and all kinds of people. The move represented much more freedom to roam the entire neighborhood. My pop still must have been holding down more than one job because he still left early and returned, at times, late in the evening. My mom wasn't seemingly too concerned about my whereabouts as much as she had been when we were living in the projects, plus I guess she probably was tired of being on constant guard and at a continuous watch of all of us. While my older sisters were at school, I wasn't in school as of yet, and this was a time when I wasn't helping Mom with hanging clothes in our new backyard. I was assigned with the mountainous task of keeping an eye on Ursula, who was two years younger than me. At that time, when you're that young, two years apart seems to be a big age difference. It didn't matter that Mom would say, "Eric Michael"—she'd call me that when she wanted my full attention—"you better keep a close watch on your sister, you understand?"

My only reply "Yes, Mom." (Hey, Mom and Pops, I'm still trying to look after them.) When I hung with Os (Ursula), I had to always hang back to make sure she was all right.

At this point, I still didn't notice any difference within us kids and the other kids in the neighborhood. One day, I went outside and saw a boy who appeared to be my size and age, so we started playing with each other. Neither of us realized that we would grow to be close in the following years, at times weathering the tough streets and all the things that kids living in a large urban area would experience. Alvin Cox was his name, and he lived at the end of the block. Alvin was nicknamed Baldy. I found out as we would soon start hanging out in the next few years that his nickname came from the close haircut he maintained year-round, especially in the summertime. It was a straight bald cut; most of us would just get a little closer cut than normal school year cuts. Alvin and I never saw ourselves as being different from each other because we both were fast, could laugh, and have fun. But also, we could scrap when confronted with the necessity. Later, we would be taught by others in the hood that there was a difference in us, a difference that took a long time for us to pay attention to, but eventually we started to notice that no matter where we went, I seemed to be viewed different or was given more attention than him because of the light skin and curly hair. The girls thought I was cute sometimes, and the dudes thought I was maybe soft. Either consideration by either group would soon cause a temporary problem between two friends who were best friends.

Throughout this book, you'll notice that I show love and respect for my father, but a special love and admiration goes out to my mom. When a person gets older and reflects on past times, they seem to see things so clear that at times they ask themselves what the concern was over this or that. Sitting here at this typewriter and pecking away, I can remember things that I'd forgotten.

Like the time when shortly after we relocated to the South Side, Mom and I were walking home from the store, and my mother said hello to a woman in the neighborhood. The lady started cussing at my mother for no reason. Mom just kept walking. I asked Mom why she did that, and my mother just stated that the lady was probably mad about something that had nothing to do with her or me. Later, I would ask my sisters the meaning of certain words, like *White bitch* or *White foreigner.* I saw how upset my sisters got that I knew them. These were bad things for a person to call my *mother!* I swore that when I got older, no one was going to talk about my mom like that around me, and I can assure you, the reader, that no one did without paying a price, with either a woman receiving a hell of a cussing out or a man or a boy getting a direct ass whooping or a threat that I could have and, without hesitation, would have carried out like a soldier who had been given an order by his superiors.

On Fridays and Saturdays, we would be allowed to stay up or outside much later than the old place. One reason is that Mom and Pops could sit on the porch and just chill and watch us all playing in the streets or in the sometimes vacant glass-filled field that was across the street. It was where later, in the following years, we would play different games. One stood out called "dead man pick 'em up," a game that was a mix between rugby, football, hockey, and boxing.

We would barbecue in the backyard, and since there were so many of us kids in the family, we could play games and always come up with some kind of activity that couldn't be practiced all the time in the projects, simply because we didn't have a yard as we did on Eighty-Second and Emerald. Whenever we wanted to go to the beach, we went to the most familiar and ironically near the Cabrini-Green projects called Northside Beach. It took us what seemed to be a long time to get there to a young person. We had to use public transportation, a bus to the L train, switch to another train up north Chicago, then another bus within a few blocks. Then we would walk an all too familiar part of the city that we chose to try and forget. Of course, when we would get to the beach, the fun was on, until we had to make a long journey back to the South Side. At times, for us kids, we would not particularly notice that Mom was considered much different from us kids and was definitely not appreciated. She was being seen with a Black man and seven (soon-to-be eight) kids that were all visibly a bit different than kids in the Black community, and it was an uncomfortable trip to the older kids and for Mom more so than us younger ones.

I thank God for allowing me this opportunity to be able to relate this story to people who have or will enter into a relationship that even in modern times is still looked at as something so different. People look at the couple and their kids as if a big green Martian was walking down the street. Whatever color a person or nationality may be, one day it won't matter within our American society (not White or Black America, just *America*)!

Pop never really said much about what it took to make a move to our house out of the projects, but Mom definitely relayed that it took "saving every dime," as she put it, and a large down payment. I've been told it was a few thousand dollars, which in these days would probably equate to four times that amount. There is no wonder my father was working day and night. He must have known to either leave now or face the possibility of something happening to one of us and him having to hurt or kill someone, which would leave the rest of us in that situation without his protection.

It's a trip to be the object of attention, seemingly on center stage at all times and being too young to realize why. No matter what things we didn't have or the feeling of not always having the most positive and strong household, we thank Mom and Pops for trying the best with a big start by giving us a better chance by moving out of the projects to Eighty-Second and Emerald.

3

St. Leo Elementary

The first few years of school were good memories. We didn't know at the time, but our parents really had to have saved and been on a tight budget to have four kids in a Catholic elementary school at the same time. Barbara was in sixth, Inge in fifth, Stefanie in third, and me in first. We all noticed the difference in how this school was ran and what our hood friends would say their school was, Gresham Elementary on Eighty-Fifth and Green, St. Leo located on Seventy-Eighth and Emerald. For one thing, we had to wear uniforms—brown slacks (dark), beige shirts with brown ties for the boys, and brown plaid skirts with vests and beige blouses for the girls. Our friends that went to public school seemed, at a young age, to have more fun and never seemed to have nowhere near as much homework as we did.

Before I type another word, I have to take a special moment and send all my love to our parents for sending us to a school that, at that particular time, was a better learning place than public schools. Attending a Catholic school instead of the neighborhood public school was telling the younger people in the hood that we thought we were better than the rest of the kids and teens. Again, it would seem to people, the older we got, that we didn't belong in the hood if we couldn't attend the schools that 98 percent of our friends did. Being mixed goes mostly unnoticed during the first couple of grades in school. Probably because everything is new and you don't pay that much attention to the negativity that surrounds you. St. Leo, now looking back, did seem to provide us with a little safer environment because there were a few kids that were also mixed or White kids (not many, but there were a few) that were living in the neighborhood.

For the most part, it seemed that directly after arriving at school until the bell rang (3:15 p.m.), you stayed busy with your classwork. My first grade appeared to be so much different than kindergarten in the projects. I really never noticed that I stood out at all. Mrs. Green was my first grade teacher, and she didn't seem to play. She would not tolerate any type of goofing off or fighting. I can remember she seemed to take a special liking to me from what I could remember, trying to encourage me oftentimes throughout the entire school day. Going to Catholic school, for the most part, was enjoyable, and I do think that this experience gave us an edge on our early academic years in early education.

I think back to waking up, and Mom and Dad would be sitting in the kitchen having their early morning ritual, which was a cup of coffee and maybe some light breakfast for Pops. Mom had toast with her coffee, and then Dad would walk up one block to Eighty-Second and Halsted to catch the bus for work. I was always one of the kids to wake early and get myself together before the bathroom got congested with girls!

My sister Stephanie was the closest in age to me, being a year and a half older. Stef would be the next to awake and get herself together and ready for school. She seemed to have less of an attitude in the morning. Once I got ready for school, I always seemed to have something to do either in the house or, weather permitting, outside of the house before leaving for school. St. Leo was just four city blocks straight up Emerald, but in most inner cities, that distance represented another hood, which at times meant fighting all the way to school. Well, there were four of us attending this Catholic school at one time. When we first moved out of Cabrini-Green, there were Barbara, Inge, Stephanie, and me. Later, there would be me, Ursula, Gretchen, and Lori (the baby of the bunch). When my older sisters were going there, there seemed to be not as much emphasis on me. I truly liked not being responsible for another sibling's safety at that time. I don't remember that type of feeling lasting for long because I've always had to be responsible for the younger ones and, to a degree, the older ones once I reached twelve or thirteen years old. I often wondered which sister would I have traded to have a little backup of a brother. Living and growing up in a big city like Chicago, brothers represented strength within any family. Most people would agree those families fortunate enough of having a few boys or even close cousins who were males could defer any possible problems, whether in school or just within the neighborhood.

St. Leo had a mixture of regular teachers and priests and nuns that taught us. This was extremely different than around our block (neighborhood). The thing that makes this a story that might be a little different from some is that not only were we different on our block from being mixed, but add to that the fact that we were attending a school that most parents wouldn't even consider if they had the money to send their kids. They wouldn't because they were mostly Baptist or Protestant or even Muslim. Once we all got used to the laughs about our uniforms and going to Catholic school, it didn't seem so bad.

The neighborhood would go through a transformation with all the Whites seeing the migration of Black families from various parts of Chicago. The public school was Gresham Elementary. All my friends attended that school. When I was in the first and second grade, I tried to keep the Eighty-Second and Emerald mentality of fighting and learning hood things away from school. But at times, especially once third grade started, I started to more and more bring this mindset of a tough exterior with the added responsibility of making sure my younger sisters were looked after. I'm sure things were just as tough for my older sisters, having no older brothers around to protect them. Once I found out exactly how much my parents had to pay each month for all of us to attend St. Leo, I knew then why things always seemed so damn tight. They paid thirty-five dollars a month for each of us, just for tuition, not to mention books, supplies, and uniforms. How they did it, I have no idea. I struggle with the little fees of public school.

St. Leo Elementary provided a seemingly more structured learning environment than what the kids on the block stated went on at

Gresham Elementary. Once, when I was in the fourth grade, Mrs. Johnson pulled me aside and said, "Eric, tell me, why do you seem like you're always ready to fight at the drop of a hat?" I remember pausing for a brief moment.

Then because of how much I respected and liked this beautiful Black (African American) woman, I then gave the truest answer I could think of to the question: "Mrs. Johnson, every time I turn around, someone is always picking on me and my sisters because we are mixed, and I'm tired of it."

As I recall, she told me to just ignore this type of unfounded ridicule unless it became a physical thing. But by that time, I was nine or ten years old, and somewhere between the fourth or fifth grade, I decided not to sit idly by while kids would choose to either verbally or physically abuse us because, in their eyes, we were different.

While in the fifth grade, the neighborhood seemed, to all of us, changed drastically over the time of one school year. I don't think it was that the hood changed so dramatically as much as we were getting older and recognizing more and more that things were getting to be more difficult. One incident stands out, and although this event happened many years ago, I can remember it well. We were on the way to school one morning, and I was trailing behind Inge and Stef, and Ursula was behind me. Inge shouted to Ursula (in this book, she is referred to as Os) to hurry up or we would leave her there. She knew we wouldn't, but it seemed to have put the necessary state of urgency within her mind because she started running up Emerald. I just started cracking up. I remember her being so mad at me for laughing so hard.

As she passed me, she tried to hit me. I couldn't even move out the way. It was funny because of how serious her face was. Anyway, as we approached Eightieth and Emerald, just two blocks away from our house and two blocks from Seventy-Eighth and Emerald and St. Leo, these dudes came up to us and started talking about what they were going to do to my sisters. Next thing I knew, we all started fighting. Although Inge and Stef could fight, my sisters weren't always matched to exchange blows with other boys. When a passerby told these dudes to leave those girls and that "half-breed" boy alone, it was well appreciated, although those words rang in and out of my head all day long. No matter who people were, they always noticed first that we were mixed or half-and-half, as we referred to ourselves. Those terms weren't so demeaning.

Overall, I still thanked our parents for letting us attend this school so as to lessen the amount of problems that me and my sisters knew we would have had to deal with by attending public school. I'm sure everyone can look back and remember some kind of ridicule from a certain source, maybe from being this way or that way. But when everyone you seem to come in contact with asks what you are or makes a big deal about color or race, after a while, you start looking for that question that even popped up with grown folks. "What are y'all, Black, White, or Spanish?"

This year was 1972, and I was in the seventh grade. I was considered on the block to be one of the fastest and considered at school to be one of the fellas not easily scared by the public school (Stagg or Oglesby) thugs who always ventured down to the Catholic school to terrorize the traditionally timid boys and girls. After all, our parents appeared to have sent us to this school either because we were very smart or to hide us from the problems of public school. In either situation, that was a very tempting allure to those who would play predators of weaker kids. In my heart and mind, I was as tough as those thugs who would come to rob and beat up classmates. After all the bullies I went through in my own hood, having to stand up for myself and my sisters, these chumps weren't thought of as any tougher than a few thugs on our block.

On this particular day, I wasn't having a very good day because I had gotten in trouble again and was sent to the school office for hitting some dude in my class at PE. I passed my sisters Ursula and Gretchen's class and stopped to make the usual funny faces at their doors. Of course, without their teacher being aware of this. I was a crossing guard sent out to my post fifteen minutes prior to the 3:15 p.m. bell. I arrived at the corner of Seventy-Eighth and Emerald, and there were already two or three public school fellas hanging out on this porch, which was not uncommon. They seemed to have more in-service meetings than we did, and it was a common thing around any hood to hang at a certain person's house whose parents would be at work or just allow the sitting and hanging out.

As I approached the corner, one of the dudes called out, "Y'all just getting out of school?"

I replied, "Yeah."

One of the fellas yelled, "What's up, White boy?"

They recognized that I was one of the dudes that would fight if needed. I didn't say anything.

Another said, "Hey, man, this punk can't hear."

Well, being the guy that I was, I stated, "Naw, man, that's yo momma that can't hear."

Why did I say that! They paused and said, "Man, he said yo momma is deaf!"

Next thing I knew, we were straight up boxing all over the corner of Seventy-Eighth and Emerald. By this time, we had drawn a crowd. Some were cheering for him, some cheering for me. We seemed to be boxing forever until one of the teachers came out and broke us up. I still remember, even years later, that when I would see these fellas at Calumet High School, there was respect that at least I stood my ground and boxed, even if to them I didn't win. So yes, we old-school fellas do know about *respect*.

Thank you again, Mom and Dad, for sending us to St. Leo Elementary. And thank you to all the faculty who might have seen how hard it was being a standout because of being mixed. A special word to Mrs. Green, my first grade teacher, who always told me I was a smart and handsome young man. And to Mrs. Johnson, that physically beautiful sixth grade teacher whose words stayed in my head about not tripping about everything people said because to her, I was a nice boy. Those bits of encouragement helped. St. Leo was a nice introduction to education for all of us.

4

Hood Games

When you grow up in most inner cities, there are always things to do and various games to play.

The South Side of Chicago wasn't any different than other parts of Chicago or, for that fact, any other urban area across these United States. In our neighborhood, we had a lot of children like most cities I imagine. We would always do something outside. In modern times, there seems to be more to do in the house for kids everywhere. They have a choice of what to watch with thirty-six to sixty or more channels, Nintendo, SaGa, or now computers to either work on or play games on as well!

I remember some of the most fun games in our hood! Even though things might have been a bit tough on our block and dealing in the city, this was a way for me to really put all the troubles in and out of the house and the daily hustles of inner-city living aside and just play as hard as I could. We all, at an early age, like everywhere else, were kicked off the basketball court. We weren't allowed to play with the big dudes in the street, in football games, or the boxing matches held in the corner across from our house.

I remember thinking, *Man, when I get bigger, I can't wait until I can play with the big boys.* For the most part, all of our hood games were just games to display people's strength or weaknesses. And believe me, you better come with everything you've got or the fellas would laugh you off the block.

I'm sure every hood had its variation of similar games. Also, every hood had its star performers and dudes that wouldn't quit until they were considered one of the best. This type of grueling display of being tenacious would later come into play and be strongly utilized without me ever giving this strong and tough mentality a second thought.

The older dudes seem to always half check out the girls who would hang out either on the sidewalks or at the park around the corner and up the street at the outside court. This park was called Garrett A. Morgan, the elementary school my younger sisters attended and the one I graduated from to go to high school.

I was about eight years old, when I actually started being able to participate in the outside games of our block. One of the first games that our hood would play if you were younger was a game called Jonny 500. Who made up this game, I have no idea. But if you were considered fast enough to star at this game, you would be considered maybe good enough to chase the ball once it went out of bounds when the bigger (twelve to fourteen years old) dudes were playing street football. This Jonny 500 was very simple to play, but of course, there was always the variation of a series of punches or kicks thrown at the person who appeared to be winning!

This particular event that we participated in was nothing short of a track-and-field game! The game went like this: two people would stand and choose people on their team that they thought would bring their team the victory. The winners cracked on the other team for sometimes days after the game took place. After the teams were chosen, half of the people would take one team and walk up the street, and the other team would walk farther down the street. They would get ready to send a person of the starting team, who simply had to run past the two or sometimes three people from the other team without being stopped, either by being grabbed or just knocked out of bounds (and I mean *knocked*). Once this person made it past these people, he and at times she would be allowed to walk back to their team's side of the street. Ultimately, the winning team was the one who had the most people not touched or stopped that made it through (no ball was used).

At this time, you, the reader, may be saying, "Where exactly is this fool going with this?" Well, let me tell you. You will hear, through my writing, me mentioning my sister Stef, who generally partook in almost all games played, probably right up to the point just before she got married (at fifteen). Stef has been my best friend all my life! She was as tough as any dude on the block!

Color never, at this point, came up. Just the fact who was the fastest, strongest, toughest, and most able to stand out athletically. Maybe that's why to this day, I am a firm believer in the participation of extracurricular activities.

The color issue or race thing seems to dwindle between athletes or even people who don't actually take part in certain games but do accept people different than themselves if the athlete performs well in that given sport. I was considered by the dudes in our hood to be extremely quick and stronghearted at everything I participated in. I grew to have the reputation of also being able to stand up to hood bullies if need be, to just be able to play on the court or field. Myself and my best friend, Alvin Cox, were the hood's fastest within our age. When I think of the hood I grew up in, I think that a few of us might have been able to go on to a higher level of sports if maybe we had a little nurturing at an early age. My three children, Eric II, Gabby (Gabrielle), and Kyle all are very adaptive to any sport and particularly basketball, because when they were young, I made sure that they were taking part in some type of physical activity. I have devoted my life to strongly encouraging my children especially and other children I come in contact with. Growing up mixed, my sisters and I were cast in roles of being better accepted if in fact we were good at something. Mine seemed to be sports. There were many games we played in the hood, like strikeout (baseball against the brick wall at the end of our block), hide-and-go-seek, rock fights, knife throwing, boxing, ice hockey (in a vacant field), pitching pennies, and shooting dice, as well as other games, some safe and some not so safe.

There was one game that stood out in my mind! That game was called *dead man pick 'em up*! This particular game, looking back, was a game that made me tough growing up in a household with all those sisters that at times argued and fussed, about what, I have no idea. Dead man pick 'em up was played simply with a football thrown in the middle of this vacant yard next to the Haney's apartment building on Emerald. This field was on the corner of Eighty-Second and Emerald and always seemed to be filled with broken glass and various debris from the previous night of gambling and drinking or fighting by the older dudes or the real hood gangsters that were in their twenties, thirties, and even older at times. We always took turns to clean up the broken glass and any items that Teddy Haney's father thought we could get hurt on while playing this game because of the nature of the game. This game was a mixture between soccer, rugby, football, and straight out boxing or wrestling. The Bible says God takes care of people and knows what we need even if we don't. Again, growing up and having no brothers in a household with seven sisters, I needed all the toughness that was thrown my way as not to be soft in an environment that would have seen this weakness six city blocks away. Well, I made it out alive, some not being so fortunate.

This chapter is a very special recollection I'm sharing with my reading audience, because the hood games were more than just regular games. They were a source of escape from all the crazy things people in my neighborhood had to deal with and the things my sisters and I had to deal with because we stood out as being different. These games taught me how to stay strong and maintain that warrior type of mentality needed as a minority, sometimes within the term *minority status*. This chapter, by far, still takes me back to a time in my mind of fun times without a lot of negative memories that came from other parts of growing up within a city and neighborhood that, through the sixties and seventies, were very turbulent, racially speaking.

Every aspect of my life as well as my sisters' lives have been affected by us being born from two people of two totally different races, nations, and very different cultures. I sit here and think about times so simple that probably made us doubt our own abilities. Like the time when Sonny Randle and James Crawford were choosing teams to play ball (I was twelve or thirteen), and they all knew at this point, being on the block for so long, that the two fastest were me and Baldy (Alvin). After everyone was chosen, they looked over at me, and James said, "Well, I guess we'll take the White boy or mixed nigga, whatever he is." And they started laughing.

I just walked up to James, who was quite older than me! "Whatever I am, I'm still the fastest on the block, punk!" (Yes, I did duck after saying that.) Later, I sat by myself on the porch and wondered why it always had to come down to this mixed thing. I quit trying to ask my parents! I never recall getting any answers.

The games in our neighborhood, for some, might have been taken lightly, but for me and for most of my sisters, we had to always perform at our best because we were under a microscope. Looking back on what type of person I am now, I truly know that although I'm older, when I go to play some ball at the gym, I still at times feel that I must perform with the same intensity as I did twenty years ago. The next time some of you are getting ready to start a pickup game in whatever sport and you see a person and you might not be sure of their nationality because of their color and especially if no one knows this person, see if you question yourself to pick this person if you aren't sure of their ability because their ethnic background isn't obvious. Throw this situation back twenty or even thirty years back, and this type of thing could really destroy a child's inner strength and self-esteem. I thank God for allowing me to tell our story!

Remember, this book is not going to make any difference to people who this interracial merger doesn't apply to unless they have someone in their family or are friends with a person dealing with this. Hopefully, after some people read this book, it will simply make them think of what things a young child must deal with because you can believe that whether at school, church, or a social function, people, even to this day (2002), still look at a biracial child or an adult and immediately form an opinion of sometimes this person is not dark enough to be easily recognized as a distinct Black (African American) person, and they may need in a certain position that requires this individual to be noticed immediately as African American, or not be White looking enough to attain a certain position!

I pray that once this book is read, it will give some insight as to what might be going through the minds of any biracial person about certain items within this book.

I enjoyed and still draw my strength needed daily from those old hood games!

5

An Early Hustle

I often considered myself a young urban businessman!

I still recall the exciting feeling of walking down Emerald Street toward the Eighty-Third and Halsted car wash! My *office*!

I just got home from school and finished my after-school chores of taking out trash, cleaning around the house, and making sure there was no trash on our walkway between the houses. Mom would often allow me to work at the car wash for a few hours and then come home and eat then do my homework! Mom had whipped and punished me quite a few times for getting my three younger sisters to the house and burning out to the car wash. After a while, I think she saw how determined I was to make some money that she worked out a deal with me. I finished my chores, and then I could hustle up some change (dollar bills) at the car wash or around the neighborhood as long as I completed my homework before I went to bed. Many days I sacrificed watching television for making a few ends that day. I also had to balance playing the hood games of Johnny 500, strikeout, against the brick wall or the infamous game of dead man pick 'em up.

This was 1970, and I had just turned ten and was in the fifth grade. I have often told my children that I worked since I was ten years old, but I actually started hustling odd and end jobs around the hood at about eight or nine. I would get up early enough to walk my father to the bus stop on Eighty-Second and Halsted!

Once I got back to the house, I would just sit on the front porch and say to myself, "I am not going to work as long hours as Dad has to work!" My father worked two jobs I think the majority of my younger years. He would leave before 6:00 a.m. to catch the CTA to the Dan Ryan to his job. It's amazing that much later in life, I found myself reverting to hood hustles, as I referred to odd jobs around our neighborhood, to make a few extra dollars.

I was cleaning basements, going to the store for people, getting race forms, raking leaves, taking people's pop bottles to the store for refunds, and getting them a paper or juice or whatever they wanted, and I got to keep the change! I quickly learned at an early age that if you get up early enough and make yourself available, people did need errands ran! At first, I probably annoyed a lot of folks, but true to any success book, *persistence* does *pay*!

The thing that drove me out of the house so early each morning for a few dollars has, throughout my life, pushed me to excel in various careers or jobs I have had. I recall how hard air traffic school was to me. I wanted to wash out (be reassigned a different job) almost every day the first two months of this six-month training, but I dug down deep for the emotional strength that drove me as a young boy hustling money on the block. Thank you, Pops, for showing me how to be committed to reaching whatever it is you want through dedication and persistence! I didn't recognize it in my dad until I had my own son at twenty years old and slowed myself down. I realized I was running from what a high school teacher told our class one day: "Sixty-five to seventy percent of you will live the same standard of living as your parents." Those damn words ring in my ears to this day some twenty plus years later! The car wash or any hustle represented to me at an early age a chance to not have to hear my mom say that we couldn't afford this or that!

Eighty-Third and Halsted was at that time a very busy corner to a young person! It didn't take long for me to also learn the pros and cons of deciding that I wanted to be a young hustler (not drugs, as referred to these days).

I didn't have any backup, as in older brothers or cousins. Of course, a couple of my older sisters did have the respect on the block as girls that never hesitated to throw down if need be. Many of the fellas on the block either had the comfort of the gangbangers knowing they had older brothers or even cousins. I stood alone. I had a couple of partners that had my back, but we were so young that none of these older thugs cared. I was too young to realize the dangers that lurked around that corner. All I saw was an opportunity to get some green, as the older dudes on the block would refer to keeping some money in your pocket/

To this day, I don't feel right if I don't have at least one hundred dollars or so in my pocket. I heard for so long that "you ain't shit if you don't keep some green in your pocket!" I also learned quickly that no matter what, things almost always came down to me being mixed as to start some type of problem. At ten years old, most things escaped my attention, so the term *ignorance is bliss* has proven to be a true statement. I would come home and show my mom my earnings. She would just stand there, looking at me for a minute, then hold her arms open. And I would give her a hug and a kiss. She really never said anything. She would just smile and start asking me about my day in school. It took years to understand that Mom felt a little troubled that I placed so much importance on hustling up a few dollars and was less excited about my school activities. I heard through my sisters and other older woman in the hood that my mom was very proud of me. Her "little working man," as she referred to me.

I could tell some of the older dudes on the corner respected me for not tripping on not having any older males other than my father around! All it took to work at this car wash was two or three dry towels and some game! "Hey, man, dry and vacuum your ride!" I must have said that statement a thousand times between 1970 to 1973 or 1974!

"Hey, White boy, mixed nigga, whatever you are, you better slow down, nigga! I need to make some of this money too!" I didn't pay much attention to those comments. I figured from all the fights I have had, what was one more?

"Hey, Eric, come here, man!" This was Bernard "Notty" Randle. I don't think Notty even knew how much confidence he gave me with a few of his words. "Eric, don't let these niggas try and scare you. You keep hustlin' up!" He would punch me in the arm and start walking away and laughing! I guess that brick-like punch to the arm was a gesture of affection, but man, did it hurt! Thanks Mr. Notty Randle!

I thought I had found a small gold mine! I would come home and have ten or twenty dollars in my pocket. Not bad for a ten-year-old! This particular Saturday morning, I got up early, did my morning chores, and headed down the street to get Alvin (Baldy) Cox out the bed so we could make some money.

I first sat on the porch as I thought about how the day would be. We would hustle at the car wash maybe around the hood. We would go to Frank's department store on Seventy-Ninth and Halsted maybe get some Converse All Stars. They were $8.95 back then! Of course, that was big money to a young person! We then would go to the Capital, a movie house on Eightieth and Halsted! A double movie was seventy-five cents for us! We would ride our bikes out of the hood all over, playing ball, pitching pennies, and just cuttin' up! We often had to, throughout the day, check in at the house!

The day ended up with me playing one of the games I mentioned earlier. The *streetlights* was my sign to get my butt home! I can't count the whooping I received from my mom having to come get me! I remember my pops being so cool if he had to get me. "Hey, Eric, it's time to get to the house!" My father didn't show any signs if he were mad, but I knew he was. It was a different story on my mom! She would walk over to me and grab my ears or pop me on the head, and with her German accent, she would say, "Eric Michael Smith, how many times have I told you to get home when the streetlights come on!" This was a joke even when I got in high school about them damn streetlights! Yeah, hahaha, fellas!

I knocked on the door, and Alvin's mother, Mrs. Lane, opened the door.

"Eric, baby, what are you doing up so early?"

"Me and Alvin are goin' to the car wash to make some money."

Mrs. Lane always asked where we were going and what we were doing. Some folks think because you live in inner cities that mothers

33

and fathers tend to care less about where or what their children are doing. That is nowhere near the truth!

"Come on in, Eric, and I will get your buddy out the bed." Mrs. Lane got Baldy out the bed and reminded him to wash up and brush his teeth. "Eric, did you eat this morning?"

"Yes, ma'am, I had some cereal!"

She walked toward the kitchen, looking back and smiling. Alvin (Baldy) came in the front with his all too familiar smile on his face and told me his mom made me an egg sandwich to take with a can of juice. We were walking out, and Alvin's mom stopped us.

"Listen, Alvin and Eric, you two be very careful at that car wash! Y'all need to look out for each other. Y'all hear me?" Mrs. Lane held her arms open for me. She always gave me a hug. Alvin, a few years later, told me his mom thought I was a good boy and a hard worker!

On the way to the car wash, we agreed on what we would do that day. We passed a couple of the older dudes on the corner.

"Y'all little niggas goin' to hustle up some money?"

Alvin and I both said yeah at the same time.

"Y'all niggas look like salt and peppa! Go ahead on, man. Make that cash!"

We always got comments on us being "salt and peppa" and hustling around our hood! We arrived at the car wash about 7:30 a.m. We were the first ones there. I recall really liking being the first ones there. It gave me a feeling that we would make *all* the money that day!

We got set up and decided that we would work as a duo, as we often did on Saturdays. This was, with no doubt, the busiest day of the week. A quick hustler could make fifteen or twenty dollars in about four or five hours. We were right on target to have a twenty-dollar day! It seemed that everyone we asked said yes. It was about eleven o'clock, and we decided to take a break and get some chips and a drink at Tommy's, a store on the corner across from the car wash. We pitched a couple of pennies, made as much as we could until about one thirty, and then we would leave. We never rode our bikes to the car wash because a chain on a bike meant nothing around here!

As we walked across the street, we started pitching a couple of pennies. A couple of dudes, a little older, about twelve maybe, said, "What's up, chumps?"

Alvin and I didn't say anything back. We just looked at them and finished pitching pennies. Our chips and drinks were finished, so we got our towels started back to work.

"Hey, salt and peppa, you niggas think y'all the only ones out here?"

"Hey, man, we just tryin' to make a few dollars."

"Both you niggas better slow down." They never did anything, but they would follow us and make other little comments. That evening, a few of us had just finished playing, so we sat on Teddy Haney's porch and started talking and laughing about the day.

"Hey, Baldy, you and Eric be makin' some dollars at the car wash! What y'all niggas gonna do with all that money?" Alvin and I just laughed and said we didn't know. Alvin and I got up and said we were going down to the house.

"Hey, Baldy, things like what happened at the car wash happen to you when I'm not around?"

"Like what, Eric?"

"You know, somebody always startin' somethin'?" I looked at Alvin's facial expression, and he started being real fidgety!

"My mom says that some people don't like it because you mixed and got good hair, but I don't care 'cause we are friends!"

I went home that night and thought about Black folks calling me and my sisters mixed, yellow, or light skinned and Whites referring to us as Blacks or Hispanics! I really don't recall our parents answering our questions about our identity, perhaps not knowing any answers themselves. Whether living in Chicago or in Leavenworth, Kansas, I and my sisters stood out as different racially. I do everything within my power to take a moment with a biracial child and offer, if needed, a piece of identity encouragement. In reality my *early hustle* was no different than any business contractor! We all *hustle* every day! It's called *earning a living*!

6

High Yellow

"Hey, Stef, are you goin' to the sweet shop [candy store] after school?"

Stef would almost always say, "Yeah, boy, I guess. You better act good in school today!" Stefanie was, at that time, my sister who looked out for me the most if for no other reason than the fact that we were so close in age, being only one and a half years older than me. Things back then seemed to be so easy for the most part, but there would always be a few in the crowd that started calling us names.

Stef would tell me to just ignore the names knowing that by an unwritten law, if I started fighting, someone might try and jump in, and she would, without question or the slightest hesitation, join in to make things a little more even. I turned the corner on Seventy-Eighth and Emerald and headed up the street toward Halsted, where the sweet shop was located. Then I heard, "Hey, y'all high yellow niggas. Don't act like y'all can't hear us!"

Before we could even respond to the all too familiar sound, they were all up on us, not close enough to actually start fighting but too close nonetheless. I looked at my sister to see whether she approved of any type of either verbal or physical retaliation. Stef gave me the look and facial gesture as to just keep walking and trying to ignore these teen thugs in hopes that they'd get bored with no response from us and leave. Well, they stopped and just ran into the sweet shop before us, looking back snarling and sticking up their middle finger.

Once we got into the sweet shop, a couple of people we knew who apparently didn't mind us being mixed or high yellow said hi and asked us how school was. They were probably speaking to my sister more than me since. Stef was the popular one in the family, especially between us, but they acknowledged me all the same, which made me feel good that someone spoke to me without first calling me names. We were just laughing and buying some penny candies. After about fifteen minutes, we ushered each other to the door, knowing it was about time for our two younger sisters to get out, and we would make the walk four blocks to a safer hood, Eighty-Second and Emerald.

These boys started calling us half-breeds, German kids, or high yellow until Stef turned and said, "Why don't you all go somewhere!" Well, I guess for the most part, they had no other entertainment except to try and bully us around. We got to the corner of Seventy-Eighth and Emerald, where St. Leo Elementary was located, and saw Gretchen and Ursula walking toward us with these dudes still running off at the mouth, with the names coming more frequent and a few curse words (cuss words). At this time, I started to lose my fear, and now my sisters were hearing these names.

Ursula and Gretchen would look at me and say, "Eric, why are those boys calling us names?" I got enraged, and as we crossed Seventy-Ninth and Emerald, where the last resemblance of any security would fade, that was the corner where the school crossing guard would be able to tell these boys to leave us alone. Although she was a White woman, she was still a grown-up, so they stopped until we all got farther toward Eightieth Street.

Once we arrived at the corner of Eightieth and Emerald, these dudes knew that if we got to the corner of Eighty-First and Emerald, we would be in our own hood. They started walking toward Stef as if they were going to hit her. And as tough as Stef was, there wasn't a chance in this world I would stand by and watch that happen. I said, "Yo momma must be close. I smell her stanky butt!"

Two of them ran at me, and I started running around a parked car in hopes to find a bottle or a stick to even the odds. I did. I grabbed a pipe I found under one of the cars and turned and started chasing them, and then I ran up on the one squaring off with Stef. He saw the pipe and took off running toward Union Street. We took off across Eighty-First Street toward our block. Once we got closer to the house, our attitudes changed to being a little more at ease, even though we heard a couple of the hood people that we didn't get along with spit out a couple of "What's up, half-breeds?" I called back to them the terms they were used to me saying: "Tell it to your momma." They didn't like that, but it was acceptable to them as calling us half-breeds were acceptable to us as a kind of greeting, I guess.

Even as I reached this age, I still cringe every time I hear a person being called high yellow, half-breed, or any name that is considered offensive to a mixed person. Listen, if you have anyone in your family or know a person whose biracial, sit down some time with them and show a little concern into their world of what I call "split identity." You could be helping them with a few encouraging words and learn something about another group of people that are minorities within society's description of minorities.

7

Garrett A. Morgan

After arriving at Morgan Elementary, it seemed as though I fit in there more than I did at St. Leo. I realized quickly that there were startling differences not only with the students and how they acted but what was allowed by the faculty. Morgan was a breath of fresh air. I wasn't thought of as some type of thug or troublemaker. The principal called me into the office and started talking, but at first I didn't hear a word she was saying. I kept staring really hard as though to follow her every word then she paused.

"Eric, are you okay?"

"Yes, Ms. Taylor."

She went on to tell me how she could relate to me being tossed out of Catholic school. She and her brothers were done the same way. Also, my older cousin, Mary Williams, was a substitute teacher, and she probably filled her in on how I was. The principal, Ms. Taylor, was no darker than me and my sisters. That is why I was staring and probably why she felt the need to tell me some dos and don'ts in her school. For the first time that I could remember, I felt like I was talking to a person who might just understand some things I had to deal with.

Ms. Taylor asked if I was interested in some sports and what my sisters were like. We spent about a full hour talking and her asking direct questions and also being as direct about fighting and various problems in this school, and no doubt she heard I had. "Eric, you

39

will enjoy being in the eighth grade here. We have some of the best teachers in the city here at Morgan. We also have new equipment, and we are proud of our school. As you probably know, living in this neighborhood for so long, that this school is very new. We've been here for two years."

I wasn't sure if she was letting me know that Morgan was as good or even better than St. Leo. It didn't matter. I felt right at home. My only concern was for my younger sisters, Ursula in the fifth grade, Gretchen in the fourth grade, and Lori Ann in the second grade. All my hood friends were there, and the other dudes that didn't stay right on our block knew me from either hustling at the car wash on Eighty-Third and Halsted or from playing ball.

My sisters didn't go out much and never really ventured off our dead-end street, so for them this new school was completely new if the kids in their classes didn't live on our block. The school still had a new smell to it and was a newly designed school from any other school I had seen, unless you ride on the L train and pass one of the colleges. I always compared it to one of the new buildings downtown. I felt extremely excited about my new school. It was a fresh start!

All the fellas from my block knew me and my reputation for being mostly cool, except when my sisters were involved or a person started talking about my mom. I was very sensitive about momma jokes or casing on my mom. All people ever joked or talked trash on was that my mom was German. I attended the school the first couple of days by myself because my parents were still getting my sisters' records and transfer info together. Those couple of days felt so easy not having to watch over my sisters that I almost wished they could have continued going to St. Leo.

I believed the excitement came from not having to wear those brown slacks and tan shirt. That was and had been our uniform since I started school in the first grade. The teachers seemed to be more at ease. I was only thirteen. Although being raised in any urban city, you are a little older mentally. Probably from the things you are exposed to, and the pace of city living is much faster than in a more rural setting.

My first day started really good, with most of my partners glad to see me going to Morgan. Also, I was going to school again with my boy, Paul Wiltz. This young brother stood a little over six feet and was very popular at Morgan. We had been classmates at St. Leo from the first grade to the fifth grade. Paul started going to Gresham Elementary then as all the other kids around my hood transferred to Morgan. The city must have built Morgan to help on the overcrowding that Gresham Elementary was plagued with. As soon as I knew I would be attending Morgan, I went by Paul's house. He lived in the next hood over on Eightieth and Union. Paul and I talked about everything, from playing ball to girls and everything in between. Paul had established himself around the hood and at Morgan as a real cool brother who only fought if he had to. People really couldn't talk much shit on Paul because this brother, as I stated, was about six feet tall, brown skinned, could play ball, dress his ass off, box well, and apparently, his family was doing okay. They had a car, and Paul dressed so sharp and always seemed to have some change in his pocket.

Some people who didn't know me probably wondered how this dude was hanging with some of the most popular and the roughest dudes at Morgan. I didn't know some of the dudes who stayed in the projects and a few dudes and girls who stayed closer to Gresham or might have even been students still at Gresham, but their parents used a family member's address so their child could attend this newly built elementary school. My very first day almost ended without an incident until after lunch, a few minutes before last hour. I was heading to my English class when I ran across Baldy (Alvin).

"Hey, Eric, what's up?"

"Nothin', Baldy. I'm heading to English class."

"Stop at the bathroom, man. I got somethin' to tell you."

"All right, I'll be right there." I wasn't sure what Baldy had to say, but he seemed more excited than normal. Baldy never hurried much and always had a smile on his face or was laughing about something. I walked into the bathroom, which was very different than St. Leo, where I was considered one of the most important people in the eighth grade. Fellas were talking, laughing, and cuttin' up.

Nobody seemed too concerned about someone coming in and telling them to chill out. The same type of activity in the hallways or in the class would have been regulated even at this more rule relaxed public school. I gave my what's up to a few fellas I had only been acquainted with and to people my boy Paul and fellas from my block had introduced me to. All the while, I was keeping in mind the words of Ms. Taylor, the principal, and other things my boys (fellas from the block) had street schooled me on.

After Baldy related to me that a few of the school's finest girls were saying how fine or how cute my Afro was, I took a piss and went to the sink and started washing my hands when this dude named Richard (Ricky) started talking to me. I couldn't really hear him. He was talking so low. I took my pick out of my pocket (always trying to keep my 'fro straight) and started picking my hair like every other brother was doing.

"What did you say?"

"I'm Ricky."

"Yeah, I'm Eric." I held my hand out to extend a greeting. Ricky stood there for what seemed to be a longer time. He was staring very intently at me. I immediately thought, *I hope and pray this dude doesn't start anything.* Not because I was scared of fighting. I had gotten so quick and good at boxing the older fellas in the hood. They would comment on my boxing skills. They would relate, "Damn, boy, I don't know if you are faster running or better at boxin', nigga!" I always felt that I had earned this rep. I quickly thought of the promise I made to my mom and the principal about staying on track to graduate from eighth grade and start high school with a good record.

"Why you actin' Black, White boy?"

Normally, I would have started fighting, but I hoped I could go through my first day without throwing a punch. A couple of my partners let Ricky's partners know they had my back. Other fellas from the block wanted to see how I would fair against a dude with a reputation of being a real tough brother who could fight well.

I chose to try and defuse this event that seemed to be very large at the moment. I heard in the background, "Yeah, White boy. What's up?"

Also, I heard from my partners, "Hey, man, this dude is mixed. He ain't all White."

Ricky came close and started to get into a boxing stand. I had literally become so good at boxing and fighting that I could assess a person's skill level and just how long it would take me to drill him from how he held his fists. After all, when you are the main attraction every day on and off your block about fighting, you can't help but get good.

"Ricky, all I really want to do is get back to class." My partners hadn't seen me back down from anyone before. They remember either seeing or hearing about the fight I had with Cecil, the hood thug, and a brother that would straight knock you out. The chanting grew more and a little louder, which apparently hyped Ricky into throwing a few punches that I bobbed and weaved with relative ease. After I saw that, I had no choice. I threw a barrage of punches and slaps. Ricky, I'm sure, didn't know what the hell had hit him. I didn't back off once I saw I could hit this dude at will. I started talking a little shit and continued to show the skills that at times I really didn't like. Ricky fell to the floor after the second attack of punches. He and his partners must have never seen a mixed or light-skinned dude box like that. A lot of dudes that were light skinned were considered soft and had no fighting skills.

My boys and some of their partners I didn't even know seemed to revel in this victory. I thought at first they were glad for me or maybe impressed with my boxing skills, but I soon learned that Ricky was the school tough guy, and being medium brown-skinned, a good dresser, and good ballplayer, he had all the girls liking him. So evidently, this yellow, half-white nigga took this dude's rep in a five-minute altercation.

On my way home and later sitting on Teddy Haney's porch, that event was the topic of discussion. Even the few dudes that didn't like me at all listened as the event was told a few times in different manners by a few different fellas. All the stories were a little different in context but with the same outcome—Ricky, one of the school's toughest brothers, had been dusted off by yours truly.

We all cracked on each other in a playful way. There was Errol and his brother, James Moore, who never missed a chance to pick a moment to get me to box with them. Errol was a year older, and James, who had already dropped out of school, was about two or three years older than I was. They let me have a moment with only looking and snarling at me! They held any bad comments. I went into the house enjoying this rare ego boosting moment on the block. I never would have thought that event allowed me and my sisters to have a good year. Other than slapping this chick named Alicia for hitting my sister Ursula, I had no other fights that year. I guess other dudes figured if this fool dusted Ricky's ass off, he wouldn't hesitate with anyone else. I enjoyed learning and having one of the best school years in my young academic adventures.

Thank you, Ms. Brown, for all the special attention you gave me and all the words of encouragement and your tough positive attitude. I cherish your words to this day. And eighth grade graduating class of 1974. Also in loving memory to Mr. Pendleton, my math teacher!

8

My Father

I refer to my father as pops throughout the book. There was never any disrespect. I grew to understand my dad. No one is faultless. and my pops had his share of issues to deal with, like growing up without his own father's guidance or the fact that he served in two foreign wars, WWII and Korea. Story related to me by my pops was that he actually spent approximately five years or more in foreign countries, which was no doubt why he married my mom, who was a beautiful blond and light blue eyed woman! I believe my father was a very wise man that could have truly made his mark in society if he didn't have to play a man's role in his family at such an early age. Pops was twelve or thirteen when he quit school and had to help with the income and care and provide the household necessities.

My earliest thoughts come from the time we were walking home from going to Northside Beach, a public beach on Chicago's North Side lakefront (Lake Michigan). As we were walking home (929 n. Hudson), cabin-green projects and some people were standing in front of our building as usual and started calling my mom and us names! I could always tell when my father was upset as any child who lived with a parent could. My pops would always twist his mouth to the side and fire up a cigarette.

Dad told us to continue walking. And as we walked ahead, I turned to see what was going on. I could tell Pops was telling these young dudes and girls something they were attentive to hearing, although from the looks on their faces, they didn't like what was being said, and a few of them probably weren't even really listening. My father was born February 2, 1921, in Mississippi.

I believe his birth name was George "Sonny" Belton. I always asked him why our last name was different than our relatives, and I can never remember being given an answer.

There has been speculation among us kids, but we never actually knew the truth. I don't know if our father ever planned to tell us all what the deal was behind the name change, but if he did, he never got around to it before he passed on, on March 27, 1987.

I owe my sense of not fearing hard work and being able to have the mental willpower to work two jobs or long hours on one job if required to my father. He showed and tried in his own way to tell us how to make it in life. That was the type of man my father was. He always talked about doing well in school and keeping a positive attitude. But there are two ways a person can say something, and I think at least for me he always talked our surroundings down because he struggled with two jobs, a small amount of sleep, and trying like hell to raise seven daughters and one son the best he knew how!

This account happened when I was ten. I had been working at the local car wash on Eighty-Third and Halsted and made about ten dollars. I was so proud I was about to burst open with excitement! I remembered that my dad might be coming home earlier than usual, and I better have the trash taken out, which was like going on military maneuvers for a ten-year-old.

I always had either a BB gun or my wrist slingshot because our trash cans were fifty-five-gallon drums located on the outside of the fence in the alley. They sat on a wooden platform my father made. You see, we had to contend with either rats or tomcats or wild dogs, and none of those filthy animals were scared of a broom or you stomping your feet or just a loud noise. This wouldn't affect these things. Only a BB shot or a rock hitting the trash cans or of course if you were good (lucky) enough to actually hit one of them. I was fortunate to have sisters take care of dishes, but boy did they get a big kick out of seeing their brother use battle techniques every night taking trash out! After the trash war, I cleaned up and headed for the kitchen table where, God bless my mother, there was always something good. I could always count on getting as much food as possible even if there wasn't a lot of extra made.

The reason was when you have at least six sisters in the house, someone is on a diet, and if they're not, you just look at one or two of them and make a remark very low under your breath so they can tell what you said but would ask for clarification.

I said, "You look like you gained some weight, but you really aren't that fat!" Well, if you lucked out and they didn't knock you off your chair, you knew it would affect their appetite. So yes, I did get my fill. At times, I still try that with my sisters now! Love y'all!

After all the nightly events and we finished our dinner, at about seven o'clock, my pops made it home, and he kind of had a ritual with cleaning up then changing and sitting in the front room, as we called our living room, with my mom fixing him up a nice plate. When you are younger, you cherish the times you can see your father or mother when they are working late hours or working two jobs and it keeps them from the house. I asked Dad how his day was and how his boss treated him. My father never complained about working or how his boss treated him! I always heard out in the street how bad the White bosses treated the workers. I really was too young to understand what the older folks would be saying on the exact treatment, but it was always so negative.

Pops would just say, "Eric, if you do your job good, they can't say anything!" I would ask how much money Dad made that day, and I don't remember him telling me. He would add with his rough way, "Son, listen. Always do the best you can in school and you won't have to worry about someone treating you bad!" I couldn't wait to tell my father that I made ten dollars today in about three and a half hours. As I got older, I thought of the things going through his mind, some joyous thoughts, some thoughts of his own worth because as I got older, I thought of how much money we hustled up on the streets with raking leaves, taking pop bottles back, working the car wash, or whatever hustle we had, mostly legal, some borderline. My pops sat there for a second and told me how proud he was of me that I would work and not complain about money. I think Pops was making between seventy-five and a hundred dollars a week. I don't even know if that was take-home pay or not. The older I got, the more respect I had for my dad, and especially my mom with rescuing us out of those damn projects then later with the move to Leavenworth, Kansas.

Dad, I believe you are in heaven because of the heart condition you had. I know now being an adult man that life and the care of a family is no small task, and you instilled in all of us the best ammunition of knowledge you had at your disposal. You gave all you knew and did everything within your power to show us how to be tough mentally and keep on going when things get rough.

I thank you for the things you showed and taught me and have let go of the things I thought were not shown or taught.

Dad, I thank you for staying with our family when a lot of men didn't and for the conversations about school or jobs I was too immature to really listen. No matter how you said it, you took the time to try and give me your best. I will always try and remember the positive things you told me. I pray you are resting in peace and awaiting Jesus's call!

9

My Mother

Anita Ingeborg Noach was born June 26, 1926, in the country of Germany. My mother talked to me about having and being able to do things I thought that only people that had money and were well-off were able to do. So I asked, "Mom, what did you come to this country for?"

Mom first looked at me, wondering why and how her only son could ask this type of question. I then asked if things were this rough (referring to my hood) in Germany. She paused as to possibly give the best answer she could.

"Honey, things were very different for me. I seemed to be more comfortable back home." My mother always referred to Germany as back home. I could never consider being any place else because obviously, I was so young, and this place I was living in was all I had ever known! When any of us moved to another city, not to mention another country with all its different customs and traditions, most of the time, we refer to the place in which we came from as home.

Mom was a very strong and opinionated woman, but she had a tender heart for those in need. Since my father worked two jobs for most of my formidable years, I learned and received most of my training from Mom.

Anita I. Noach had, to a degree, accomplished certain goals in life prior to getting married and moving to the United States!

Our mother, at a very early age, qualified to be a backup swimmer at the same Olympic games that Jessie Owens took the gold medal in track-and-field in, the 1936 Olympics. I can still remember the first time I heard this. I felt so proud that I was about to burst open. Mom never said much about that, only that her father made her stick with the training and that her training was very intense.

She would refer to some times in her life that stood out in her memory, when things were maybe harsher within her country. But I never got the impression it touched home so much. Maybe her father and mother kept the outside world from entering the household. My mother relived at times the atrocities of the war (WWII) and what changes were brought on her family, primarily her father. She related to me one day after I was upset with some people calling us and her names about Hitler followers. She saw I was extremely upset and she said, "Eric, you should be proud to know that your grandfather, who you were named after [Erich Noach] would never join Adolf Hitler's Nazi organization. He had to leave Germany since he wouldn't become a Nazi or a Nazi sympathizer and worked in South Africa as a welder. So, honey, when the kids or any people say anything about your family and Hitler, don't get upset. They just don't know."

Our whole life, no matter where we went, seemed to revolve around my mom and dad and us being biracial. Certain things, even to a young observer, seemed to change for the family when I was in the fourth grade. I wasn't sure why until some years later, once I understood the time I was in the fourth grade was the same time I recall Dr. Martin Luther King was assassinated. We always studied about famous as well as infamous Black leaders, whether they were current or in history. Dr. King is and was revered as one of the premier civil rights leaders. I personally truly admired this man, Dr. King, for standing his ground and trying as did Malcolm X and others to right the wrongs and trying to level the playing field of life for African Americans.

So to remember the bad treatment and outright disrespect my mom underwent throughout these troubled times simply because of being White and being considered a foreigner is painful. Although, she, as anyone would, hate the things people would say or try and do to her, she never, in my presence, spoke against or taught any of her children to dislike a certain people.

Mom always took the time and would sit me down and say, "Eric, when you get older, people are going to give you a hard time because of your color, who your mom is, or even White people for who you father is. But, honey, stay strong and don't view people as being bad because a few people act ignorant toward you for any of the reasons I've given you. Eric, we all belong to the human *race*!"

I have dedicated this book in remembrance of Dad and Mom, but there is a special attention to my mom for the strong character she instilled in all of us and relentless attitude to obtain our goals. Additionally, for the continuous sacrificing of herself and her basic material needs so we could have the best start in life! Mom, I know you are with me and my sisters. Thank you, and we love you and think of you daily. God bless you!

10

Calumet High

One of the first times I passed this high school must have been about 1970. I remember this because I had to walk to Foster Park for baseball tryouts. Foster Park was on Eighty-Second and Troop. Calumet was on Eighty-Second and Carpenter. The school was absolutely the largest school I could, at that time, remember ever seeing. The school campus was about four city blocks. We (the fellas) always commented that Calumet resembled a prison, with all the guards and boarded-up windows!

I must have passed Calumet more than a thousand times prior to actually being a student there. If I wasn't going past the school to attend some type of tryout at Foster Park or just swimming at the park, then I was going past Calumet from football practice since I played on the flag football team in the seventh grade.

Once I graduated from eighth grade at Morgan Elementary, I was selected to attend a new high school out on 132nd and Halsted, Carver High, a beautiful brand-new high school that was supposedly designed for the serious-minded student. I was fourteen and really trying to come into my own personality. I tried playing the guitar and various other things. My mom especially tried encouraging me to finish, so this was the perfect school for me. I thought the school had auto mechanics and was deemed as the school to attend if you thought you wanted to really achieve at something other than being a thug or hustler. I attended Carver High for only two weeks when

I saw that this school was as high-tech as it was. It was no different than the things I heard about Calumet. The only difference was that at Calumet, I knew quite a few people. At Carver it was only a partner named Tony from Morgan. Carver was only open to those students who managed to attain a B average the last year of elementary. So being selected to attend Carver had been considered a privilege.

There were problems with gangs every day trying to rob those of us that weren't from that area in Argyle Gardens, another set of projects. On this particular day, Tony and I were talking about what had been going on with these robberies and that we would not settle for our hard-earned money we hustled up so hard to be just taken like we were some punks! It really started to hit me that I actually drew negative attention to myself or anyone that was with me by being mixed when this gangbanger was on the bus, on the way home after school was looking around, and our eyes met.

"What's up, punk?" I never answered him. I just looked away, realizing Tony and I had no type of backup, and unless I had no choice, I needed to avoid this bullshit!

"Hey, White boy, you hear me?" Again, this dude was far enough away, and the bus was crowded, so I played him off, really hoping he might just leave me alone or something. All I had to do was make it to the train stop at Ninety-Fifth and the Dan Ryan expressway. Tony and I lived within the same area, just a few blocks out our hood on Emerald. Tony lived in the projects on Eighty-Fifth and Vincens.

Tony quit talking to this girl and said, "Eric, man, is this dude talkin' to you?"

Tony really never seemed to pay attention to all this mixed, Black, White, or color thing! I only really new Tony from Morgan and playing ball at Morgan's courts. I always enjoyed Tony's conversations. He never talked about me being yellow, mixed, or anything other than what had been happening around our hoods or getting real jobs, girls, if we would be going to college. I always could just be myself and have fun.

"Yeah, Tony, this dude is trippin' about me being mixed. He thinks I'm White!"

"Hey, man, I don't know who you are talkin' about. My partner ain't no White boy! Nigga, he's mixed. He's from around my way!" Tony never went for bad, but you could tell this average-looking brother was no stranger to trouble. After all, like Tony would say, "Man, me and brothers don't trip on this gangbanging shit. Eric, we just deal with it when it comes our way!"

"Nigga, who you think you talkin' to!"

"Hey, man, my boy is right. I'm not White. I'm mixed!"

Before anything else could be said, it caught the attention of this older-looking brother that I noticed sitting a few seats over. This dude had been sitting there the last few times we had gotten on the bus to go home. The dude, who first started to get my attention with calling me a White boy, made his way past a couple of people with this hard ass look on his face!

"Hey, man, back up and leave these niggas alone!" To my astonishment, not only did this troublemaking fool back off, but it seemed to quiet the rest of the gangbangers on the bus down. Tony just kept talking to this girl like nothing happened. I, on the other hand, had put my brass knuckles my father made me back in my pocket. I played this off as though I didn't really think twice about what had just transpired, all the time heart was pounding so loud I thought the girl next to me would be able to hear my heart or perhaps be able to feel the seat throbbing. I thought to myself, *I'm going to Calumet. At least it is in my hood, and a few of the gangbangers there would know me!* Other than the dude who started this trouble, looking at me crazy, the rest of the thirty-minute bus ride to the Dan Ryan was relatively uneventful. Once these dudes got off the bus a few stops before we reached our train transfer, I really relaxed.

"All right, we at the Dan Ryan," the bus driver hollered. As I started to get off, I was thinking about this quiet brother who, with a few words, defused a potential bad situation.

"Hey, man, you got a minute?" Tony looked at me and nodded as to let me know he had my back if needed.

"Yeah, what's up?"

"Hey, I know y'all ain't no punks [no scarred dudes], man. I'm Earl. I'm a junior at Carver. I stay around Eighty-Seventh and State."

Here was this brother who was about six feet, give or take an inch, and average skin color (medium brown), who might have been held back a grade or two because he had a goatee and looked like he was out of high school. "I know most of them bangers they run with the stones [Blackstone rangers]. They really not tough unless they got niggas outnumbered. Anyway, if I can help, let me know.

"Hey, man, wouldn't it be easier on you if you went to Calumet? I heard y'all say you stay on Emerald!"

At first, I was really skeptical about this dude. "Why would you say that?" All the while, I knew what he meant. I just wanted to hear him say it.

"I mean, 'cause you mixed and all."

Tony, not saying a thing, just looked at this dude as though he didn't understand. Again, my boy Tony never made any distinction about my color. He always treated me like I was just another partner of his.

"Man, all I wanted to do was enjoy this new school like everyone else. It seems like it always comes down to me being mixed, not just around here but back at the crib [my block] too."

"I know what you be going thru, 'cause my cousin is mixed, and people always be tryin' to trip on him 'cause he's real yellow and got good hair. Hey, y'all fellas be easy, and remember, I'm Earl. And if I'm around, they won't trip."

We exchanged handshakes and nodded to Earl as he walked off. Tony and I talked about how cool Earl seemed, but we reminded each other that we should kind of watch our own backs. Strangers are always kept at distance where we come from. I made my mind right then and there that I was going to tell Mom and Pops I really needed to enroll at Calumet. My reason would be that we lived on Eighty-Second and Emerald, and Calumet was on Eighty-Second and Carpenter. It was only minutes away, even by foot, and I knew a lot of people I'd be in school with. I waited till about the time the news came on (9:00 p.m.) and asked them if they had a few minutes. Mom and Pops had seen, since I started high school, that I seemed to be a little more serious-minded toward my classwork.

Once actually enrolled and attending classes at Calumet, things didn't seem nowhere as bad as what my sisters said about it and also people off the block. One reason was because I knew so many people from just living in the neighborhood since we moved from Cabrini-Green. There were people that I didn't even know went to Calumet that I had been friends or acquaintances with in the past.

Although it didn't take long to realize why this school was considered one of the toughest schools around. Calumet had three floors of classrooms, one of the largest cafeterias in the district, several gyms, and an indoor pool. This school might have, at one time in the past, been considered a very good school, but again it resembled a correctional facility. There were a lot of windows boarded up, chains on the doors, and police and security guards on duty while school was in. Imagine being fourteen, average height (about five-seven), yellow with a big curly Afro, attending this all (98 percent) Black school of about three thousand students.

Again, growing up remembering certain rough things from Cabrini then growing up on Emerald and dealing with the discrimination of being mixed in an all-Black area made the things at Calumet easier to deal with, but it was still a rough school. At this age, everything was blown out of proportion any way because of your hormones and becoming aware of things around you more. I have said this throughout my book. I respect what our parents did in raising us, but at the same time, when everything you do and every move you make is scrutinized and ridiculed only because of the color of your skin, well, if you aren't strong, you can crack under that type of pressure.

I walked up to the gym door before PE started and read this letter on the door in larger than normal print: BASKETBALL TRYOUTS! A couple of partners asked if I was going to try out. I said, "Yeah, why not."

When the day came to practice, I was in the locker room dressing, and this older dude from the varsity squad walked up to me. "Hey, Red, are you really going to try out?"

I had become accustomed to hearing someone call me *Red* directly or refer to me or one of my sisters as Red. I hated that term.

The term *red* in my mind was a put-down. And depending on what type of mood I was in, I would just answer a question or statement or just say, "My name is Eric, not Red." I was so excited about these basketball tryouts that I really just looked up at him for a few seconds and said, "Yeah!"

"Man, Coach don't like no half-breeds."

I remember quickly thinking to myself, *Who in the hell does this funny looking big head punk think he is?* "I don't really care what he likes. I plan to make the team."

"All right, White boy, mixed nigga. Don't get so mad!" Thank God that dude walked out because I would have gotten suspended and might beaten up that day. Once dressed, I tried to put the statement made by this varsity player out of my mind. I walked into the gym, only to notice about one hundred others with the same idea as me—to make a twelve-man roster. As I walked across the court for one of the first times, I remember feeling like I was truly in the wrong place. I quickly scanned the benches for familiar faces as to grab a seat near some partners. I absolutely remember thinking of that event in various time in my adult life as the memory had no doubt made me a little better at handling everything from test taking to interviews.

I was a little early, as were those of us sitting there. I guess all of us were thinking the same thing. We might be late for some classes, but we definitely didn't want to be late for tryouts and bring any negative thought from the coaches to ourselves. After putting my name and homeroom on this paper attached to a clipboard, the paper asked two other questions: last school attended and position trying out for. The coaches had a brief meeting as they were apparently grouping guys in the positions on the paper. I remember my name being called by this tall brother who had the appearance of a ballplayer. After assembling about thirty-four of us, the coach introduced himself. "My name is coach Chambers, and I will be working with guards. I want to tell you all this. I don't have time for instructional ball. I'm here to assemble the guards needed for our freshman-sophomore team."

I did pretty well, only missing a couple of layups. I thought I had gotten the coach's attention with my quickness! After the first day for tryouts, we all started walking toward the locker room. A few dudes I knew and a few I didn't know told me I seemed to be the fastest one out of the group of guards trying out. I felt like if all these dudes noticed me, certainly Coach Chambers saw me. I was feeling so excited I was about to bust.

"Hey, Red. Hey, red!" I thought at first this dude who I talked to in the locker room was getting ready to tell me the same things the other fellas had told me, about my speed on the court. As I turned, all I saw was Coach Chambers and the varsity coach I knew but never met. I was hoping to God one of these coaches didn't refer to me in that manner. After all, I just bust a gut in a two-and-a-half-hour practice. I froze and just looked down when Coach Chambers said it again. "Hey, Red, come here!"

It seemed as though I was moving in slow motion. I finally reached where they were at and looked up. Coach Chambers just looked at me, and Coach Lee introduced himself. "Hi, I'm Coach Lee, the varsity coach."

"Hi, Coach. I'm Eric." My mind was moving about a million miles a minute, trying to think why I was singled out. I finally got the courage to ask why I was called. Coach Lee asked me if I had played ball for Morgan. I said no. Coach Chambers asked why I hadn't played. I told him I had been cut from the team. Coach Lee looked at the roster as to get my real name, knowing himself that Red wasn't my real name.

"Eric, maybe you'll be ready next year. Coach Chambers only has three or four positions for guards, and we already have our guards picked out. Hey, track season will be here soon." I felt as though someone had just punched me in the head!

I can tell you, the reader, that I carried that pain around with me for years. I looked up at these men I held in high of regards as a person held their ministers. After that incident, I fought more in school and even started to smoke. I started to drink with the fellas, and my schoolwork went to barely passing. A few teachers and my counselor would talk to me, but they had so many students to deal with that they couldn't spend any real time trying to find out what the hell was wrong with me. Calumet, I believe, had some of the best teachers in the city, but I imagine the complacency tended to set in when they saw the school seemingly being ran by thugs and some students who really didn't give a damn about an education.

I really don't know how I got out of my freshmen year with the grades and a few suspensions on top of that. Maybe the school had to pass so many of us at that time! I actually wasn't nowhere near as problematic as some of the other students. A few friends that had flunked their freshman year just dropped out and hung out, joined the disciples, or started hustling. I left Chicago the summer after my freshman year to work as a kitchen help at camp holiday, a summer camp program for inner-city youths from Chicago. Since I attended camp a few years, my mom pleaded with Children's Memorial Hospital's social workers, who were familiar with us since we were young, to give me a summer job and get me off the block for a minute! It truly was one of the best experiences of my teen life.

When I came back to Calumet, I was an inch taller and a little more mature. People noticed I was cooler acting, dressed a little better, 'fro neater, and I talked less. I went to all my classes and even participated in class a lot more. I had regained my focus of college or perhaps a new idea of joining the military as an option. Through all my classwork and still hustling around my neighborhood, I held this desire and drive to not only make the team (basketball) my sophomore year but to start on it!

I saw both coaches throughout my gym classes. I never really said much and tried not to be noticed by either coach, for I grew to dislike them for what they had put me through the year past. I had heard the reason I didn't make the team was that the coaches thought that as fast as I was and as tenacious and aggressive as I was, I would be too soft to make the team. Again, they had referred to me being yellow or a half-breed as synonymous as soft!

I acted cool, all the while waiting to get on the court for tryouts. You see, I had not only gotten an inch taller but also a little street smarter. I felt as though I had something to prove to these coaches who thought me being mixed made me soft, as well as me knowing that all the hot summer workouts and early morning runs would now pay off!

As I walked toward the gym, I saw on the large double doors BASKETBALL TRYOUTS! I had one of the only White PE teachers in our school, and as I dressed for gym class, he called me over.

"Hey, Smith, will you be trying out for the school basketball team?"

"Yeah, Mr. Dean."

"That's good, Smith. I think you'll make it."

I acted as though his words meant very little to me, but actually, I was boosted to an even higher feeling of my skills.

Myself, James Taylor, Paul Wiltz, and several other fellas dressed and walked on the court. We were sophomores now and had much more confidence and familiarity with our school as well as our skills and abilities. Coach Chambers slightly acknowledged me, only nodding in a familiar way. Once on the court, I could tell in the corner of my eyes the coaches were admiring my improvements of being faster, jumping higher, being more controlled, and picking dudes dribble from them so frequently they preferred to pass the ball when I approached them to D them up instead of dribbling to get by me!

Fellas were giving me fives all around the gym. There were approximately one hundred freshman and sophomore boys trying out for this twelve-man roster, again! Every day, there were cuts being made. Some fellas that you thought were pretty good ballers were cut. I made it a point to not say anything to the coaches unless asked. Occasionally, Coach Lee made it into the gym after his varsity players concluded their practice and watched our tryouts, giving nods to fellas who made a good pass or scored a basket. I went out of my way to show no interest in his presence. I could tell after I did a good pass or stole the ball from someone that him and Coach Chambers appeared surprised at either me coming back out a year later or the fact that I had shown this type of improvement in my game.

To conclude this chapter, I can tell you that I did, in fact, make the final cut. I made the team! Cuts were made every day for one week, and about eighty or ninety boys were being released from tryouts without making the team. Coach Chambers taught me a lot that brief season before we left Chicago and moved to Leavenworth, Kansas. The most important thing Coach Chambers told me was that he apologized for thinking that I wouldn't be tough enough for his team because I was mixed. He said he would never make that mistake again.

"Color doesn't matter, Eric. Be strong and be careful in your new school." Calumet was tough, but the school made me emotionally a stronger person.

11

Sentenced to Leavenworth

The day was January 4, 1976, when we arrived in Leavenworth, Kansas. We had lived in Chicago all of our lives and only knew city type of living. My mom asked if I had a minute a few days before I left with my father. My father and I, at that time, didn't get along at all. My father's way of encouraging us, unfortunately, was to put us down or many times the people we hung out with. I have realized in having my own children that being a parent isn't as easy as some people make it out to be. I know my father and especially my mother did the absolute best job they could have done, and I truly hope that I can do as well as they did.

"Eric, I know you and your father have your differences, but please try and talk with him. Son, your dad loves you very much."

"Mom, you know I try and talk with Dad, but he's always so negative on everything. I really think he doesn't even like me." My mom just paused and gave me that all too familiar look that I would disappoint her if I didn't do what she asked of me. "Okay, Mom. I promise I'll try. I will."

"Son, this move to Leavenworth is going to be good for all of us, you'll see."

I kept these words fresh in my mind the entire time my father and I sat on that long bus ride to Kansas. I was no stranger to seeing country type of living with the bus and train rides to Camp Holiday located in Lake Geneva, Wisconsin. This camp was about a three or four-hour bus ride into Wisconsin from Chicago. We would all just sit there in amazement, going past that open country space and those farms, and it seemed that people out there lived a lot slower. And I could always remember no one being worried about someone robbing them, or for that fact, a lot of quietness. When I was between ten and about thirteen, I would often daydream about living in a place where people just treated you the way you acted or maybe not always have something to say because of your skin color.

I had friends once we moved to Kansas tell me that they were the only Blacks in their entire school for years, and perhaps the only thing that changed was their parents that moved to an area that was racially mixed. My sisters and I could relate. When Pops and I arrived in Leavenworth, we were met by a friend of his he was stationed with when he and Mom arrived at Ft. Leavenworth a couple of years before me and my sister Stefanie was born. My two older sisters were born in Leavenworth, Barbara and Inge. Anita was the oldest and had been born in Germany.

Sonny and Naomi Griffin were a seemingly nice couple. Sonny, who drove a new car and worked at the federal penitentiary, always dressed nice and had a very cool way about himself. Naomi was the type of woman who was hard to figure out. She was very pleasant but seemed to be checking us kids out *all* the time, especially me. I was the oldest out of the kids that were still living at home and made the move to Leavenworth. I always liked Naomi. She was often one of the only friends my mom had, along with Mrs. Fish. Naomi told us to call her by her first name, something we were never allowed to do growing up. We always called grown folks by their last names.

I think I was in total shock the first couple of days in Leavenworth. This town looked like something you would have seen in a movie from the fifties or sixties. For a brief moment, my father and I would actually talk and laugh. It was something we hadn't done in years. I wasn't distracted by thinking of what type of hustle I would be doing that day, and I'm sure my father, at that moment, wasn't worried about my safety or me getting into some kind of trouble. We were on a mission to find a house to rent. Leavenworth had no real bad parts, especially since the population including the fort was only about forty thousand. It felt like we had that many people in our neighborhood. Pops and I would laugh at people commenting on the traffic or would tell us that up north Leavenworth had some bad crime spots. Sonny would drive us around looking for rental houses, and he and my father would try to talk over my head about the drinking and gambling that they participated in when they both were stationed here in the fifties. I never said much. I just let them think I wasn't paying attention. All the while, I was studying what type of hustle I could do here. I was so used to being able to make twenty or thirty dollars every day and not really going out of my hood. Leavenworth's Black population was about a fifth of the town's population, and I soon found out that in a town this size, everyone new everyone and just about what everyone was doing, good and the bad. Once we found a house on Cleveland Terrace, we phoned home and relayed the good news to my mom and my sisters. They were all very excited and said they would start packing immediately.

I didn't know at that time, but this move would turn out just like my mom had said. All I knew was that I was leaving a place I lived in all my life, and even with the gangs, the tough school, and the big city living, I learned to hustle up a few dollars, and from the time I was ten, I never had to ask my parents for any money. There are so many things Chicago offered to a young dude who, like myself, wasn't afraid to get up and ask around who needed something done.

We took the Greyhound bus back to Chicago to help pack and return to Leavenworth to live. As soon as I got back on the block after only being gone about five days, I looked around and saw how different things were. Here you had to stay alert no matter where you were or what you were doing. In Leavenworth, I attempted to relate to a few partners that were interested that the difference was like night was from day. I spent the next few days packing and getting things done to move. I was always allowed to go and come relatively easy, but since we were moving, my father seemed to really not even ask where I was going or if I was going to hang out with those thugs, as he referred to my friends who actually had the same interest in going to college or joining the military after graduation. I visited everyone that I was cool with, and we reminisced for a while and shared brief thoughts on how things would be around the way without their mixed partner being in the hood. We laughed, and when we started to get sentimental, we started cracking on each other more than usual so we could hide the emotional event of leaving lifelong friends. I can still remember sitting on our porch and just thinking of all the good as well as bad times we went through on our dead-end street, on our block. The last couple of years had been some of the most fun as well as hard probably because I started really noticing everything within my surroundings. The older I had gotten, the more I noticed that this color or race thing wasn't in our imagination. This was always with us, either directly targeted at us or in the news some way. I don't think my father ever knew how much I envied him being medium brown in complexion. There were a lot of times that I would have rather been all White or all Black. The one thing that Leavenworth had was a mixture of people. It took a while getting used to going to school with Whites. It wasn't that I was prejudiced against Whites, but I hated the fact that here in this smaller town, people seemed to always refer to you by who your family was or what they owned or didn't own. My sisters and I found ourselves at times more on guard in small Leavenworth than in the big city of Chicago. Leavenworth didn't have the gangs that Chicago had and virtually no crime, but it actually had as much color or race dividing, if not more.

Once we got settled in and got ready to enroll into this new school, there was a mountain of changes, especially for me since I would be attending midsemester of my sophomore year. My parents totally enjoyed this move. I stopped being selfish as much as a teenager could be and viewed this move for a while through my mom's eyes. Here in Leavenworth, my mom wasn't this object of hatred. I have described my mother throughout this book with having light blond hair and bluish-gray eyes. The very typical German woman. My seven sisters and I (the only boy) often spoke of people treating us different than other classmates or friends we hung out with. For anyone who has had the experience of being raised within the inner city, they could testify that there are situations you are exposed to that a person wouldn't have to deal with in a small city or rural living. I decided that I would, as much as I could, leave Chicago's mentality within the boundaries of that city. It didn't take long for me to realize that we had moved from the troubled city life any family faces, but the fact of being mixed would remain with us.

The very first day of school at Leavenworth Senior High School was a nightmare for me. My mom went with me to enroll me. The principal stated that he had gotten some info back about me getting into fights at Calumet. Here sat a man that, out of his own mouth, said he was born and raised and remained in a small town all his life and wouldn't pretend to know what big city living was like, but that he would not tolerate any troublemakers in his school. Mr. Jacka was a tall heavyset man in his mid to late fifties. "You seem to have quite a reputation for fighting."

I said nothing. I just sat there with the fiercest look of contempt on my face. Mr. Jacka and I had a sort of stare off for what seemed to be a long time that was appropriately interrupted by my mom. "Mr. Jacka, my son had only been protecting either himself or his sisters. Did the school tell you that?" My mom's accent was always there, although I could only recognize it when I was intently listening to her. My mom always looked at our side first. Our dad seemed to side or believe others first. I was really happy Mom was enrolling me. I wouldn't be sure if my father would have divulged any incriminating information about my past.

"Mrs. Smith, I understand what you're telling me, but the fact remains that this high school is not a Chicago school. I hope your son will fit in here and do well."

"Eric will do well. He's a bright boy."

"Oh, also, Mrs. Smith, Eric being a sophomore must take ROTC."

I swear I almost came out of my chair when this big, fat, and obviously prejudiced man made that statement. My mom was not familiar with ROTC. I knew in Calumet that the people that took this class were deemed as squares or people who had no type of athletic skills.

"Mom, I can't take this class." Before my mom could even answer, Mr. Jacka took pleasure in telling us that for sophomores, this wasn't an option. It was mandatory.

"You also must cut your hair." My large curly Afro was the same in my mind as the Bible relates the story of Samson's strength being in his hair. This was my total identity. After my mom enrolled me, he gave me the option of starting school that day or going home and returning the next day. The principal suggested I should go this afternoon in search of a barber and return to school *neat*, as he put it. This man showed no interest in me making an adjustment to this different environment!

Neither of us spoke the first couple of blocks as we walked home since we didn't own a car, and Leavenworth wasn't equipped with the type of public transportation we had become used to. I am forty-two years old, and I still get choked up about what happened on the way home and once Mom and I arrived at the house. I couldn't bring myself to tell my mom what thoughts were roaming through my head. I held so much love and respect for my mother, I would go out of my way to make her smile and not to get her upset. After all, she had a couple of my older sisters that had brought her a lot of pain from the trouble and situations they had gotten themselves into. Finally, within a few blocks of the house, the silence was broken by my mom.

"Eric, I know things are different for you here, but I still think this move was better for all of you." I thought even more respectfully toward my mom. I was thinking that the move was most beneficial for my mom's peace of mind and safety as well.

"Mom, I am really tryin', but everywhere I turn, these people are trippin' on me about something. If it's not these grown folks, it's a few people I've met. I know you all like it here, but I can't make any money, and I'm tired of thinking I have to prove I'm tough all over again just because I'm mixed." I took a few steps in silence. I was looking down, waiting in response to my statement from my mother. Mom was just walking with her head down. I looked closer and raised my mom's head up and saw tears. Before I could say anything, she apologized for us kids always having received ridicule from being mixed.

"Son, at times I wish I could reverse time and not put this on you kids. I'm sorry, Eric." Right there, I decided to, at whatever the cost, hang in there with my mom and my three sisters. I would sacrifice or suppress any notions I held in secret of returning to Chicago and finishing school at my rough but familiar Calumet High.

"Mom, don't ever say anything like that. It isn't your fault people treat us any different. I wouldn't want any other mother in the world." I dried her tears away, and she flashed that smile that kept me thinking positive about life in general. I did go get my hair cut that afternoon! Quite a lot too. I packed the rest under my ROTC hat. I put grease and put a stocking cap on the night before our weekly uniform day, held every Wednesday. I'm sure the instructors knew, from seeing me the rest of the week's school days, having more of a 'fro than on uniform day. I didn't take ROTC the rest of my high school years.

My returning to Leavenworth High my junior year would prove to be one of the most internal struggles I can recall. I had left Leavenworth June 1, 1976, for Camp Holiday to work another summer as kitchen help. This was my second year being invited back to work at this camp. My summer went by, and I had a lot of fun. I mostly worked on my basketball game and enjoyed the outdoor life in Lake Geneva, Wisconsin. I didn't leave camp until about the twentieth of August. From there, I stopped in Chicago for a couple of days. I stayed on the block with Alvin Cox. I had only been gone from Chicago for about eight months, and everything had changed, or perhaps I had drastically changed. I don't believe in mere coincidence. My view changed after working at Camp Holiday of around 90 percent White college students and hearing the goals they shared and the fun they always spoke of about college life. I had a focus on going to college far greater than I did before I left. Alvin gave me the scoop on the hood activities since I had been gone.

"Eric, man, these dudes are getting crazy around here. James Spencer shot and killed Levi. Nicky tried to shoot Greg Stokes, ran all up on the niggas porch!"

"Damn, Baldy, what's up with these fools?"

"Man, everybody is strapped now. You picked a good time to move."

After we walked around the hood and said what's up to a few people, we ended up back on the corner (Eighty-Second and Emerald). This was about six or seven o'clock. I was just standing there, laughing about what someone had said, when a younger dude from a couple of blocks over around Green Street asked me why I was standing here on *their* corner talking shit! All the while, his hand was in his jacket pocket. At first, a fear crept over me. I hadn't felt it before, a sense of me having too much going for me to either get shot or end up, if I even still had a gun with me, shooting this fool. I hadn't had those type of thoughts living here before.

"Hey, nigga. You better shut up before this half-breed nigga does somethin' to you!"

I briefly looked at Errold Moore, who made that statement to this young thug and quickly turned back to this dude. I barely remember him. He was probably no more than fourteen years old. He and I stared at each other for a moment with total silence from the fellas on the corner. This young thug-looking brother obviously thought about the statement made by Errold Moore, an older thug from Emerald, because he backed down and held his hand out to shake. I slowly, cautious of showing any weakness, shook his hand. This handshake, for the moment, worked as a temporary truce. We all went right back to joking and laughing, all the while knowing this dude could have shot me if Errold hadn't made that remark.

Errold Moore and I had been true adversaries since the Moore family moved on the block in 1971. He and his brother, James, would talk about me nonstop. They called me everything from White boy, half-breed, to Hitler's niggas. I actually grew tough on my block from these two dudes who I thought must have sat up at night thinking of names to call me. So the comment Errold made to this up-and-coming young thug wasn't because he shared any likeness for me but strictly because even Errold and his brother, James, knew I would fight to the end with whoever I had to. After all, they knew I didn't back down from them, so I wouldn't hesitate throwing down with this younger and smaller dude who couldn't even touch their reputation for being tough. A few of us got together to briefly relive a couple of funny times around the block before I told them I had to run around the corner and holler at Bobby Ragsdale, who wasn't at home when I stopped by earlier.

Bobby and I shared the most in common with each other. We both never looked for trouble, but when it came our way, we dealt with it. Bobby was one year older than me, and I'm not sure when we really started hanging real tough, but it had been a few years ago, about 1973. Bobby had two sisters, Lawanna and Tawanna, twins. If I recall right, it was Lawanna who liked me. These twins were thick and fine, with dark brown skin and a pretty shape. Quintin, Bobby's younger brother, made comments all the time of me being mixed. And a few times, he would say, "What's up, White boy?" and then run.

Bobby would just look at me and say, "Don't trip, Eric. That boy ain't got no sense."

I never let on like I even thought about it. I had become a little more mature on how I handled someone inquiring about what nationality I and my sisters were. Or the fact that someone just wanted to comment on us having no real identity. I would let these comments made by Bobby's younger brother go right past me. The biggest reason in Quintin's situation was that Bobby was one of my closest partners. Through the years, he proved to have my back no matter what the odds were or how bad the situation.

I left the next morning on the Amtrak for Kansas City, where I would be glad to see my moms and even glad to see Pops. I had about eight or nine hours to think on that ride, and I thought about how wild things had gotten back home in Chicago and decided right then and there to make Leavenworth home. I figured my mom and my sisters needed me. I never returned to Chicago until I went back to visit ten years later, about 1988. I tried to forget the way I was and all the rough times growing up there. The first sixteen years of my life had been very hard, and it all seemed to center around being biracial. Once back in Leavenworth, I felt at times like an undercover nice student who tried to get along. All the while, I felt so hostile toward anyone who made fun of me or my sisters.

The next two years would prove to be the most life-changing time in my life, even in comparison to present-day events. I did play ball for the Leavenworth Pioneers, and I did graduate in May 1978 on time. I started college in the fall of 1978 and was hired on at Hallmark Cards. Not bad for completing two years and a few days of my Leavenworth sentence.

12

Trying to Fit In

The month was June, the year 1978. I had just graduated and was really feeling a sense of accomplishment. After all, I was the second one in my family to actually graduate. Out of my four older sisters, Anita was the only one to actually graduate and attend college. Barbara, Inge, and Stefanie had dropped out before they completed high school. My father's house rules seemed to be more than I could stand. Although he changed my curfew to 2:00 a.m., I pushed it to the limit almost every night. I acted disrespectful, maybe not being mouthy or drinking or smoking around the house. I always watched my mouth around my mother. I have learned that being a parent means enforcing the peace and solid welfare within your home. I had purchased my first car, a 1967 Buick LeSabre. Me and my boy, Ronnie Fields, washed and waxed that long green Buick until the faded green turned into a shiny faded green car. I was coming into my own. I just wasn't sure a lot of times what that was. It seemed at times as though I was as mixed in behavior as I was in nationality. I loved the library and visiting museums and things like that, but I also felt a strong desire to fit in somewhere.

I really started hanging out more. That hanging out led to thinking I was grown, and I was steadily ignoring the advice my father was giving me. My father was the type to put some things down constantly. Now that I'm grown with kids of my own, I realize all he was trying to do was keep us, mainly me since I was his only son, from maybe making mistakes he made or just bad decisions.

Finishing high school was a completion of a milestone and the start of young adult life. When people fall in love or maybe just decide to have sex with the possibility of children being born, they should and often don't think of the things these children will go through. At that time, I disliked being in the middle and not having a real sense of fitting in. All through high school, the first thing students, teachers, coaches, or school officials would try and do was figure out what race my sisters and I was. I never ever remember anyone every asking us what our mother or father was.

"Excuse me, would you mind if I ask you a question?" I knew what the question was almost 100 percent of the time. I had often grown so accustomed to questions like those that I grew more tolerable. When we were younger and I would come home and tell my parents of these type of questions, the answer was almost as if they had scripted it.

Mom and Dad referred to people, mostly other kids, as being ignorant or rude. As I have matured and reached an age of truly knowing who and what I am, I have had time to reflect on my growing up. I don't think a lot of people were being rude as much as us just being different from them. We had good hair, or so it was called, and were much lighter skinned! I heard a radio program back then and was too immature to call in and give my opinion. The talk show was on mixed families and how they got along in their communities.

I can still remember the talk show and some of the comments that a few people on the panel made back then. Considering that time was 1978, and being eighteen years old, a young person wasn't as articulate as they wanted to be. I remember thinking that these grown-ups were all talking and not really addressing the real issue of actually being biracial and what children or young adults are experiencing in their daily lives. Probably most mixed children know the first thing a lot of people tend to ask is "What are you?" or "What are you mixed with?"

All I heard were grown-ups talking about how they felt. I have either heard or seen various shows throughout the years, and all are or seemed to be centered around what the parents are going through. If a child is mixed, especially with a Black parent and the child has taken the color from the White parent, then a lot of people seem to either think the child or person is Hispanic. I thought that now I'm about to start college, surely I won't have to go through this "What are you?" routine. *Wrong*! You guessed it. *I did!*

The summer after graduation went relatively at a normal pace, with no outstanding events other than being excited about accomplishing getting out of high school (*legally*)! I actually received a diploma. Me, Randy Fiends, and Rodney Windom were to attend Emporia State College. This particular college was considered one of the best division two teachers' college around. We were all very excited and for that moment very focused on our college futures.

Rodney Windom's father was, at that time, an Army lieutenant colonel on active duty stationed at Ft. Leavenworth. I often wondered why Rodney liked running with me and a few of the fellas that were considered polite, well dressed, weed-and-wine partakers that never looked for problems at the same time didn't run from any. I knew that Randy Fields, his brother Ronnie, Lee Carrol, Randal Wallace, and myself came from normal everyday working families just struggling to live a decent life. Rodney's father was stationed at Ft. Leavenworth and to this day is an officer training college! His dad had a different lifestyle of not only being active duty army but being a high-ranking Black officer. I figured out he must like feeling that he was just one of the boys even if he had certain things and was privileged to a way of life we had no clue at that time existed. I had been dating Rochelle Vann, my children's mother in present day, for about seven months. I didn't let on to the other fellas that I was punking out of going to Emporia State because I thought that two and a half hours was too far to be away from my girlfriend. Like I said, the summer had its concerts we all attended and house parties we went to. I held down a couple of jobs to keep some money in my pockets and some petro in my ride. It never failed any time I or we went to some function and someone didn't know me or know of me. They would inquire of my ethnic background. Sometimes, if I was in a playful mood, I would act as though I was some type of Hispanic or from Cuba, or they would ask if I was Puerto Rican. I often said, "Español si, no Englais." I don't know any Spanish, can't you tell? I would just clown like that!

Many people that will read this book will not understand the difficulties of fitting in or many times the feeling that you don't belong. There have been plenty of times I have been with a few friends (mostly Black), and we were discriminated against because of being Black. I remember being in a department store as a teenager, and this manager walked up to me. "Hey, son, are you with those black kids?" I couldn't believe he dared separate me from them. I was no more than a few feet from a few partners of mine!

I quickly answered as to hope he wouldn't tell us we had to leave! "Yes, sir, we are looking around."

"Well, look somewhere else. You need to tell them you all must leave or I'll call security."

I recall thinking, *Why is this dude acting like this? We have bought in this store plenty of times!* We all would hustle up money from either the car wash or some other neighborhood hustle and then come up to Frank's Department Store and buy our Converse All Stars or other gear! I didn't want any trouble because I did know of some other thugs in the hood that would steal a few small items! When I did this manager's dirty work and told the fellas we had to leave, at first everyone started walking out with just mumbling of the injustice we had just been dished out.

All of a sudden, a couple of the fellas started calling this White man "hunky, stupid White boy" and various other names, along with a couple of non-direct threats. "Man, wait till we catch yo ass out-side!" We knew we would be back in the store buying as soon as we gathered up enough money! The store manager practiced this routine! Once out of the store, a few fellas turned on me.

"Eric, they wouldn't of thrown you out if our Black asses wasn't in there."

"Hey, man, I'm in the same boat as y'all!"

"Yeah, right, you know they consider you a White boy."

I distinctly remember that statement not bothering me as much. I glanced at a few of their faces and looked at my longest and closest partner, Alvin Cox (Baldy), and saw he was just nodding in agreement with everyone else. I was about thirteen or fourteen, and that entire day burned a memory of when things came down to it and no matter what I thought or how I thought we were all the same, my partners, classmates, and even adults like that store manager always seemed to separate us.

My parents never wanted to address this biracial thing. Maybe they themselves had problems with it, or maybe just like a parent with the responsibility of talking to their child about sex, the subject of interracial marriage was uncomfortable. There was another time I recall being discriminated against from my Black side. I had moved to Leavenworth, and I still laugh at this particular occasion. Me and a few fellas were going to this local park on Ft. Leavenworth, Patch Community Center.

At this time, I was a sophomore attending Leavenworth High. Mike Dixon, James Wills, Dennis, and myself called next game.

"Hey, Eric, you runnin' with yo White partners?"

Before I could even respond, this fool was just being silly. "Hey, man, y'all know Eric is one of them peck-a-woods too!" These dudes that were talking trash mostly did it in fun. I hadn't heard anyone refer to me as a peck-a-wood.

I started laughing and really cuttin' up when James and Dennis, both being White, said "Are we going to play ball or what?" One of the fellas who started crackin' on us mocked them in a voice that resembled a TV announcer, pronouncing each and every word very intensely.

"ARE WE GOING TO PLAY BALL OR WHAT?" The whole episode was funny to some of us, but we all realized that on this basketball court where there were no managers, no refs, no principals, or not one grown person that might regulate this capping (put downs or dozens session), no one could stop our laughing! Whereas that manager back in Chicago ruled that store especially to young teens, these brothers outnumbered and ruled this basketball court. Living in Leavenworth, I had a few friends that were White. I learned that as tough as some of these White boys were, they openly conceded to brothers in the streets.

At times, people didn't know my ethnic background. I actually had fun with the mistaken identity. "Hey, White boy, you want to box first then we can play ball?"

"You mean I have to box you before I can play ball?" I lowered my voice and spoke very precisely and deliberately, like White people do.

"Yeah, if you can outbox me, you can run with us."

Like I stated earlier in this book, being the object of difference in a large urban area, you learn to be tough or stay in the house. "Well, don't hurt me or anything."

"Sho you right, White boy!" Jay was this young man's name. I won't tell his last name, but I'm sure the fellas reading this book will quickly identify him. We started boxing, and after a few very quick jabs and right punches to the head, the fellas around stopped playing ball, started looking at this untelevised, no payday boxing match. After that brief altercation that thank God didn't last long and didn't escalate to anything else, I really didn't have much trouble. After all, Jay was considered one of the toughest young Black dudes around, even within the fellas that were out of school.

"Damn, man, don't no White boy know how to fight like that."

"Hey, man, you mixed or something?"

"Yeah, I'm mixed."

All of a sudden, I had an instant reputation of being a fighter. Oh, a few fellas always seemed to crack on me being a White boy or mixed when they wanted to either cap on me or were really mad and wanted to provoke me to throw down.

If you have someone in your family, cousin, niece, nephew, or even a close friend, try and take a moment to find out how sensitive this person feels about not really having a true sense of belonging or maybe feeling like they just don't *fit in*.

13

Different Shades of Color

"Daddy, why do we have different colors?"

"Well, Gabby [short for Gabrielle], there are a lot of colors so we can appreciate different things God has given us."

I prided myself on taking time with my children, especially when they were asking questions. As I was about to go into this so-called "father knows best" philosophical and probably long-drawn info session with this beautiful and very inquisitive daughter of mine, she interrupted me. "No, Daddy, I'm talking about you, Mom, Mikey [my oldest son Eric], me, and Kyle [the baby boy]."

At first, I thought, *Why is she asking this type of question?* Gabby was very direct in her questions. We sat there looking at each other for a few seconds, not saying a word. She no doubt wondered why this question stumped this man, her dad, when I always tried to have an answer or seem to know where to find one. Our children often have nicknames, and kids, I found out, realize that when Mom, Dad, or perhaps grandparents call them by their birth name instead of the family given nicknames, their full and complete attention is required.

"Gabrielle, a lot of families have different shades of color and are from the same mom and dad. Did you hear something in school today?"

Eric M. Smith II (Mikey) and Gabby attended the same grade school in Leavenworth, Kansas. Mikey was in the fifth grade. Gabby was in the second, and Kyle was one year old. My wife and I never tried to talk anyone down because of his or her color or let the kids think this light and dark thing, a lot of black families go through, wasn't important on the outside. It most importantly meant absolutely nothing within our household. I was not going to avoid any questions my children asked. I often initiated certain topics, like why some people are married and others are divorced, why some kids have stepparents. Like I said, I tried to share information on various topics that young kids or older kids are curious about. I truly believe our parents, as did most parents a generation ago, weren't comfortable answering certain questions or sharing information on this different color thing.

After Gabby and I sat at the dining room table, where homework and school projects had often been worked on, I asked Gabby various questions, and I didn't feel I was receiving the answers I either wanted to hear or perhaps answers I was hoping to hear.

I knew Mikey would be downstairs in the family room I so proudly fixed up. "Mikey, Eric Michael, where are you?" He couldn't hear me over the volume while watching *Cartoon Express*. As I entered in the family room, Mikey looked up and immediately asked if I needed anything. Here sat this handsome, medium brown-skinned little dude who always tried to imitate me at this age.

"Hey, son, I'd like to talk to you for a few. Turn the TV down."

Mikey often thought maybe he was in some type of trouble. No, not that he was a problem child. He just loved to play and joke around, which led to some of his teachers sending a repetitive note home that read, "Eric is doing pretty good in his classwork, although he gets a little rowdy. He is not in trouble and didn't do anything to receive a detention period. I [Mrs. So-and-So] just wanted to touch base with you. Sincerely, Mrs. So-and-So."

I as well as Mikey's mom would scratch our heads and say, "Is this a bad note or a good one?"

"Mikey, you are not in any trouble. And no, son, your teacher didn't call. I just thought you would be able to let me know how things were going for you and Gabby in school. Son, I'll get straight to the point. Gabby asked me something on skin color today, and I thought some kids might be trying to mess with your sister."

"Dad, you know I won't let anybody bother Gabby. All I heard was that this teacher at recess asked Gabby if me and her had the same mom and dad." Mikey and I talked about the comment the teacher made. This particular teacher was one of my favorite teachers, so after I talked with my son, I went back upstairs and directly asked Gabby about what the teacher said to her that sparked this sudden interest about what color she was. I talked it over with my wife, after her initial response of any educator responsible for the care and learning of our children asking a second grader a question she should have asked us on one of the various school activities one or both of us frequently attended.

I didn't have to report for work until about one o'clock in the afternoon this particular day, so after consulting with my wife, I decided to visit with this teacher and let her know she can ask us any questions about this matter but not to ask our young children. I always went to the kid's school dressed well as to not embarrass my children. After all, this was a business meeting between Gabby's teacher and me.

I thought throughout the night about me and my sisters attending school and the occurrences, whether considered problems or just things that happened. The kids and I had breakfast every morning. This time with them gave me the opportunity to encourage them to have a good day in school. In addition, I used this time to ask very targeted questions about whatever they consider important in their lives.

"Gabby, I'm going to take a minute with your teacher and see how things are going."

"Okay, Daddy, that's fine."

"Dad, are you going to see my teachers?"

"No, son, your teacher sent a note home a couple of days ago and said you are doing really well. I'm really proud of you." I turned away as Mikey reminded me of myself and my younger days. Gabby never was concerned about me or her mother coming up to school. She knew, even at her young age, her teachers always spoke very highly of her. I looked over at Mikey, and he was tearing up his breakfast as usual. He seemed to relax after I told him what the note from school said.

After strapping Kyle in the car seat and Mikey and Gabby going through their usual "who sits in the front seat" routine, we were off. I just listened as Mikey and Gabby laugh at the smile their brother Kyle always held on his face. They would take turns pushing down on his forehead and saying he looked like Mike Tyson. I reminded Mikey that he was going to school to learn, not just participate in PE class and not to clown around so much and to pay attention to the teachers. We would drop Kyle off first, which always took an extra minute or two. Kyle, being only one year old, had all of us watching over him so closely.

Once Kyle had been dropped off at his daycare, I often spend the next ten-minute ride regulating Gabby and Mikey from picking at each other. We arrived at Muncie Elementary. Normally I would just go through the car rider's line, where parents dropped their children off one car after another, dropping kids off and driving off until school was over and reversing the procedure. This day, I pulled into the visitor's parking area. I hugged and shook Mikey's hand. That always made him feel older as related to me. Gabby, all the while, was smiling and holding my hand tight. Gabby would hug and kiss me every day before and after school. I looked forward to this school trip daily. It often helped me through a rough day. I ushered Gabby off to class and told her I had to stop by the office and get a visitor's pass to see her teacher. After receiving my pass, I assured the vice principal I would only take a moment with Mrs. Evans. As I said earlier, I liked her way of teaching. Mrs. Evans seemed to really care for her students and particularly my daughter.

"Hello, Mr. Smith, how are you?"

"I'm fine, Mrs. Evans. I won't take but a moment. I wanted to talk to you about a question you asked Gabrielle about if her and her brother were real brother and sister or stepsiblings."

The look on her face told me she was very uncomfortable about me asking her this. "Well, Mr. Smith, I assure you I meant nothing by this. Is there a problem?"

"Well, to be truthful with you, there is no real problem. Gabrielle asked me about people in our family being different colors. When I asked her why this mattered to her, she told me you asked her if her and her brother had the same parents."

"Mr. Smith, I apologize to you and your wife, as well as to Gabrielle." I reminded myself quickly that I was here to make sure she kept Gabby's best interest at heart while Gabby was in the class, not to hold some type of lesson to this grown person.

"May I ask, Mrs. Evans, what prompted this question?" Again, she had this extreme expression on her face. Then the moment of truth happened for both of us.

"Mr. Smith, I think you know how much I care for Gabrielle."

"Mrs. Evans, you are, without a doubt, one of the best teachers I have run across in my children's school years this far. I wanted to be able to answer any questions as well as find out why my daughter asked me about color in our family. She has never been concerned about this before now."

Mrs. Evans paused, searching for the correct answer. "Your son Eric and Gabrielle are different in color, so I guess I just wanted to know if they were stepbrother and sister as many of our students are. I hope you can forgive me for being so ignorant on this matter."

I was totally knocked off my feet. I was surprised she came clean with her answer. Although, I was relieved that she did. Lots of Black families have various skin tones within the same family by the same biological parents. Just like some Whites have children with blond hair, and other children in the household by the same parents have darker hair.

"Mrs. Evans, you are not ignorant. Again, my wife and I really enjoy Gabrielle being in your class. I and my wife are the biological parents of Eric, Gabrielle, and Kyle, their younger brother. My only concern is that my children remain close, and I don't ever want one of them to think there is a difference between them because one is darker or lighter than the other."

"I do apologize, Mr. Smith."

"Well, Mrs. Evans, I hope you have a good day, and please don't let Gabrielle know I've come for this reason. I told her I came to

check on how she was doing. She really enjoys being in your class."
As I walked out of the school and toward my car, I couldn't help but
think that although this is 1990, approximately thirty plus years after
the start of the civil rights movement, color of skin seemed to be such
an issue.

We, at times, once the kids had gotten a little older, would joke
about the five different shades of color we had within our household.
Rochelle, my wife, was a dark reddish brown, me being light, bright,
and damn near White (as some people say). Mikey was a medium
brown-skinned little brother, Gabby a light caramel color, and Kyle
slightly darker than Gabby. Like I said, five different shades in our
household.

Once I joined the Air Force, I would have drill sergeants with
very little tact say, "Airman, what are you?"

This would give me the opportunity to mess with these
authorized bullies, as they were basic training instructors. "DRILL
SERGEANTS!"

"Drill Sergeant, I am BLACK!" You could tell by the hesitation
these trained professional men or women exhibited that there stood
this bald, shaved, yellow trainee with no facial hair telling them he
was Black. I hope if this perplexing situation comes up after one of
these people have read my book, they will be able to shed some light
(excuse the pun) on this subject. I heard a mixed young man tell
his mom, when a Black and White person have children, they make
Mexican-looking people. I have been mistaken for everything including Cuban, Hispanic, White, and from some people, not sure if I'm
a light-skinned Black. Often people are either selected or rejected by
simply being of a different shade of color.

14

White, Black, Other

The first time I can really remember having to select my race was in the eighth grade, and I was about to graduate. There had been other surveys in previous grades, but they were to be taken home for one of my parents to complete. The teacher doing this particular survey told us the information received from them would be used to get better equipment and new books for Morgan Elementary.

"I realize, students, that by the time we get updated equipment, you all will be almost through your freshman year in high school, but your younger family members as well as other students will benefit from this survey." I asked if this was to be taken home. "No, Eric, you must fill these out in class, and they must be returned to the office today."

The questions asked were very general and pretty easy to understand. I recall there being about thirty-five to forty questions overall. I remember very distinctly the question that I sat there and looked at for quite some time:

Check one of the following: WHITE_____ BLACK_____ HISPANIC_____ AMERICAN INDIAN_____ OTHER_____.

I sat there just staring at this question. The teacher administering this survey wasn't one of our eighth grade teachers. She apparently had been randomly selected to fulfill this extra duty. I tried to move on and answer the other questions, but I kept coming back to this question as I was emotionally drawn to it as a moth to a flame.

This teacher, once the survey had gotten underway, would occasionally answer various questions from students who needed assistance. I tried very hard not to establish eye contact with this teacher as she sat on the corner of the desk and scanned the classroom for raised hands or students that appeared to not be completing the survey. I recall moving around in my chair and nervously repositioning myself at my desk. All of a sudden, I looked up toward the front of the classroom, and my eyes met the teacher's, and she started walking toward me. I don't recall her name, but I can still recall how she looked. This teacher, I can recall, must be old, about thirty something. She was brown skinned and very shapely as the fellas, myself included, talked about how fine and built she was. She moved about slowly and with such confidence. This teacher reminded me of one of those fine sisters that *Ebony* magazine displayed each month. She arrived at my desk and, with a very pretty smile, leaned forward.

"Eric Smith, right?"

"Yes, ma'am."

"Eric, you seem to be having some difficulty. Is there something I can help you with?" I was known around my hood and at school as this mixed dude who wasn't really shy but didn't stand out in a crowd except for always being the brightest (color wise, haha).

I didn't want to draw any attention to myself because I tried to show I was always overly confident about everything. I wasn't sure how this teacher would respond to me not knowing which answer to circle. I thought she might make some type of unwanted comment about me not knowing what nationality I was. Some kids at school or within my neighborhood might not be good in schoolwork or good at some type of sport, but they never had any questions about their nationality or were the object of some ridicule because of being mixed. Some partners of mine were talked about because they were very dark skinned or real light skinned, but they were still considered to be *Black*. All I wanted was to be able to blend in and not stand out all the time!

This teacher turned my survey paper around and quickly saw other questions before and after the race question had been answered, but no circle had been drawn around any answer to that question.

I immediately froze as I realized she saw I had a problem answering this question.

"Eric, I know you see me in the halls. I'm one of the fifth grade teachers, and I have had one of your younger sisters in class this year." I didn't know why she was sharing that with me. All I wanted to do was to get past this question and be through with this survey.

This teacher, whoever and wherever she is, helped me make up my mind that particular day with who or what I have become up to this day. "Eric, I know you and your sisters must, at times, have it rough growing up around here and going to an all-Black school, but let me tell you that society, especially White America, thinks of you all as *Black*. I know you all get very tired of ignorant people making unnecessary comments on your color or your hair or whatever they can come up with. When I look at you, I see a very handsome, light-skinned, very strong young black man, okay?"

It's funny how one comment from one person can change a person's life. All the time she was talking to me, she never raised her voice past a slight whisper. "Yes, ma'am. And thank you very much." That teacher always, from that point on, would call me by my name every time she saw me. She would make comments like "You're looking sharp today, Eric!" She would be one of the few people that commented on how my Afro was cut. "Mr. Smith, you must of gotten a haircut this weekend. Your 'fro is looking good!" She made me feel as if I actually belonged here.

Like I said, I don't remember her name. I often think of how much her comments helped me feel good about myself and who or what I was. I would recall her words! From then on, all my school, job, or military records showed either circled or written BLACK, AFRICAN AMERICAN, or AFRICAN GERMAN AMERICAN.

The advice I now give to younger or older people who are biracial is don't get caught up in all this *Black, White, or other stuff*. We have one God and are part of his human *race*.

Our parents must have thought that if they didn't address the biracial situation, then maybe their kids would be all right. Although I owe my very existence to my mom and dad, you must, as parents or guardians, instill an *identity* in your child. Share with your children both cultures. Please don't try and either ignore or downplay the importance both cultures have to offer in your child's upbringing.

Maybe in the future, *color* or nationality won't matter, but it does at present (the year being 2002). Perhaps there will be a future census taken to see the ages or how many males or females there are in this country and not be concerned about a different race selection!

15

Misunderstood

"Good morning, Bob. How are you today?"

"What's up, Bob? You all right?"

"Hey, Jim, these guys have talent!"

"Yo, Jim, these boys got mad skills!"

The above statements have the exact same meaning, and no one is trying to put anyone down. The greeting and the statement about some ballplayers are simply expressed by two different cultures or possibly by two different generations. Being of two different nationalities and trying all through my life to be as objective as I could be, I realize at a very early age that even within my own household growing up, our parents found themselves meaning the exact same thing, but the words just came out different. I recall the sitcom *Sanford and Son* with Red Foxx and Demond Wilson starring as father and son, owners and operators of a junkyard located in Los Angeles (Watts). I don't think I missed many shows. I still watch the old show on whatever cable channel it plays on. There was one particular part where these two actors playing cops often checked in on Fred Sanford (Red Foxx) and his borderline legal operation. One cop was White, the other Black. The White cop never understood Fred or Lamont, Fred's son (Demond Wilson). The Black cop translated almost every statement from Fred and Lamont to the White cop.

The White cop was portrayed as a stiff shirt, very educated, intolerable, and unbending in the ways of Black people, their language, and often the way we (not all, but some) run businesses. The Black cop was portrayed as a cool brother who knew his way around the streets of Watts but also was trying very hard to do his job as a police officer. I didn't dislike the White cop. I just liked the way the Black cop did his job. The Black cop wasn't as concerned about the small things Fred Sanford was doing. His character was made to seem like he understood that most people in the ghetto had a side hustle— selling food stamps, hustling various things just to use a word our own government uses, providing *supplemental income.*

I have seen this within my own household when I was growing up. A person might give a White person a greeting or even a compliment, and they completely come unglued thinking that the statement was some type of slang used to make fun or put them down.

There are very distinct differences within the two races. I have lived it. I realize Black people in this country are far different than our relatives two or three generations ago. Look at old television clippings and see how subdued and benign Black folks had to come across. Whites were more aggressive could say and do whatever they wanted. Fast forward the television to current times. Black people are allowed to act natural, not as though they are scripted.

I went to go see the movie *Training Day* with one of my favorite actors, Denzel Washington. I normally attended the matinee showing because you get in at a discounted price. In addition, you don't have to worry about young folks being loud and commenting on the movie as if they're move critic. This particular day, I worked a little harder the previous night and slept a little longer in the day and missed the early showing. I didn't have my son Kyle, who I often would pick up after school. And if I didn't have to work that night, he would spend a night, and I would take him back to school the next day. I decided to go get something to eat and treat myself to a movie. I thought, *Well, I worked enough overtime last week. I get paid tomorrow. I can afford a movie tonight even if I have to pay a regular seven-dollar ticket price.* (It was much cheaper than some cities.) The movie started at seven thirty. I knew it would be crowded because the movie had just come out the previous Friday. I was right. It was jam-packed, not a vacant seat in the place. No sooner had the movie started than these young Black teenagers started being loud and commenting on almost every scene. I saw a White man, I thought in his late thirties, walk up to the young people with this long flashlight and pointed at them and said, "If you all aren't quiet, you'll be required to leave."

The young people were about two rows from me. They started cussing loud, and I knew the next step would be him getting the police officers in the lobby, and that meant this situation could be explosive. I stopped the theater manager and asked if I might speak with these young people before he did anything. He looked at me with a very inquisitive look and, with a shaky voice, said, "Yes, I don't think it will do any good, but you may try."

I turned and walked up to the young people and leaned over. "How are you all? Listen, I know you all are just having some fun, but the manager is about to have you all escorted out by those police officers in the lobby. I told him you all are okay just enjoying the movie. I'd like to ask you if you all could please hold it down a little."

They looked at me for a second, and then one of the young men held out his hand. We shook hands. "Good lookin' out!" The movie went on with no other interruptions. I realize that the young people were out of line, making loud comments, but in most situations, a little tact goes long way. The manager had every right in doing his job, but he needed to realize that these Blacks would take his words as aggressive in nature and might respond in a negative way.

I was at work one night, and a few of us decided to go over to the waffle house and have lunch (at 2:00 a.m.). There were four of us—myself, two other brothers, and a White coworker. After we ordered, I noticed a table with some Whites, and they were getting loud with the waitress. There was another table of some younger Blacks, two young ladies and two younger brothers. They were simply laughing a little louder than normal. Now I myself and the other brothers noticed one of the manager's pointing toward the table of Blacks and completely ignoring the table held by the Whites and all their loud comments and the disturbance they were causing.

As I ate my food, I watched intently to see how this would be handled. The Whites at the one table got increasingly loud and disruptive as it appeared that they had been drinking. Finally, the one manager walked slowly toward the Blacks and asked if they could please keep the noise down. Me and this brother named Phill couldn't believe this shit was going down like this. After all, this was the same kind of thing that the White managers at our job across the street did on a daily basis. I felt like bum-rushing this redneck and knocking him out. I looked at Phil, knowing how this dude hated the way our every action was evaluated and misunderstood on our job. We looked at each other and said we wouldn't get involved. We let these dudes fight their own battle. The young Blacks were probably really hungry after an obvious night out on the town from the way they were dressed, or perhaps they didn't want to start anything because of them being in the company of these young ladies. Still, nothing was said to the obnoxious table of Whites.

We finished our meal, and as we walked to the register to pay, myself and the other two brothers just stared intently at the Whites being loud at the table, subconsciously wanting them to say something. I walked up to the Blacks at the table and told them they all looked real sharp and to be *real* careful. They nodded, as no doubt they knew I was telling them to watch themselves in this establishment.

There are a variety of issues each race can dwell on. It seems as though people's actions are interpreted wrongly. White people are more apt to pay close attention and follow rules and regulations to the T without any variance. Black people are more inclined to try and bend the rules and be a little more flexible in situations, with the idea of being more agreeable.

As I have gotten older and much more comfortable about who I am, I enjoyed various conversations with people on race relations. Again, it isn't as if I consider myself some all-knowing professor on this interracial or even biracial thing. I just know what me and my sisters have lived through. Also, quite a few other mixed people have shared similar opinions. Someone once told me that race relations have gotten much better within the last thirty years. I thought, I didn't feel like it was necessary to argue a statement like that. Just pick up a newspaper!

A person would have to live a very remote life and have no access to modern broadcasting, whether television or radio, to truly believe that. The company I am employed with contracts for Burlington Northern Santa Fe Railroad. The crew I was assigned to work with that particular night had about an hour before we could unload these trailers and containers from the railcars, so we went to the crane pad (break room). There were about eight of us in there. I was the only Black person in the room. I went to wash my hands and face, came back, and just sat quietly with my hard hat over my face when all of a sudden, the trivial conversation turned from work to how they really disliked the Blacks on the ramp. At first, I started to jump up, but I chose to listen as long as I could take their comments. They might have thought I was asleep. Some would question my nationality because of me being so light skinned.

"I am sick of them so-called brothers on the ramp. Always laughin' loud and not doing their damn work."

"Yeah, ain't not one of them no damn good."

I startled a few of them when I literally jumped out of my chair. I have learned how to control my actions, but these were White boys that I thought were always laughing in our faces, sharing lunches and other things that coworkers do.

"What in the hell is wrong with y'all backwoods chumps? How y'all gonna sit there and talk about us on the ramp like that?" I wasn't out of control. I had been waiting for an opportunity to let some of these prejudiced dudes know exactly what side of the fence I was on. A couple of them sat there, looking stupid. This one extremely hateful dude came to his feet (on the other side of the table).

"You know, Eric, I'm tired of you brothers thinking y'all don't have to carry your weight around here!"

I glanced across the room and noticed most of them having their heads down while a few looked me straight in the eye, nodding in agreement with this redneck's comment. I actually respected this particular individual not only for speaking his mind but how he handled himself on the ramp. His name was Tracy, and I had seen his kind before. He never made any misconceptions about his views on working with Blacks. Tracy as well as others on the ramp lived in a small town in Missouri. Some related that the only time they came into contact with any Black people was here at work.

"Tracy, you are so racist that no matter how hard we work around here, you will say we are lazy or we don't do our jobs. You guys want us to drive around this ramp and remain quiet unless you want us to say something. Hey, man, someone needs to let you in on the news. *Slavery* is over with, and this ain't no plantation, *boss!*"

Tracy lit a cigarette and just sat back down and told one of the workers, "Deal the cards, bubba."

I grabbed my hard hat and walked out. I really wasn't mad. I was more relieved that I finally got the chance to tell a few of these good ole boys what position I took. I understood being this age and having a lot of experiences around a variety of workers that these particular Whites were no different than the ones I worked for at a corporate headquarters. They dressed well, held college degrees, but they were never vocal of their prejudiced thoughts. The only way you could tell the way that corporate level was looking at things were their hiring and promotion procedures. That's why I respected Tracy.

I know that Black people in general are on the defense when it comes down to interacting with Whites. *Affirmative actions* was made into law for a reason. I had the opportunity to work in a corporate setting as well as within a blue-collar environment. Black people want more opportunities for advancement and to be treated with more respect at work. You simply cannot approach Black people as you do Whites, whether in public or on the work front.

White people are more serious and give off the impression as though they are more skilled or more professional. Black people, throughout the history of this country, had to laugh more in the face of adversity just to keep one's sanity. Keep in mind, God views us the same!

I realize I am biracial. In the past, I wrestled with my opinions and views on various issues. I had a Black father, and I was raised in a predominantly Black area. So yes, I always held views and opinions as a Black man. Everyone may not feel like this. My opinion.

People can marry who they want, but consider the difference within the races when the possibility of children exist. Teach your children about both races and all the differences culturally. Experts relay that within one more generation, the mixed thing or biracial people might be the majority race.

A time may come when people are not so *misunderstood*.

16

Outcast

This particular chapter was probably the most difficult one to write because it caused so many different thoughts to arise. As far back as I can remember, I desired a happy and peaceful family. I'm sure other families have similar stories, but I'm not writing about other families. I'm writing about me and mine.

"Hey, Dad, why don't we have family reunions or have our uncles and cousins over to visit like my friends have?"

"Son, people work, and as far as your cousins, they live across the city and don't like coming to a different neighborhood."

My father didn't talk much about why we seemed to have very little contact with cousins we knew and some cousins we hadn't seen in so long that we forgot they even existed. Now, Mom, on the other hand, was not shy at all about correcting Pops from time to time.

"Robert, you know your family doesn't want anything to do with us because of me." We didn't notice our mom's German accent until she was upset about something. Boy oh boy, when our mother was upset, her accent came alive, and we noticed what others in our hood would say.

"Man, Eric, we can't believe you don't notice y'alls mom's accent!"

The older I got, the more I noticed that others in our hood would sit around and talk about the family reunions or family get-togethers. Also, people would talk about doing this or that with extended family members.

"Dad, can I call your brother, Uncle Shaza, or Aunt Bay?"

"What about cousin Charles and nim?" (slang for them).

"Eric, son, why are you so hardheaded? Why don't you just go outside?"

I started heading outside to rip and run on the block. I had to have been around thirteen, because I recall thinking about finishing up eighth grade and what high school I would be attending.

"Eric Michael, come here for a moment!"

My mom passed away in 1989, thirteen years ago, and even though I'm forty-two now, I still hear her calling me at times. She had a very distinctive motherly way of commanding your attention when she called. Whenever my mom called and wanted me to know she meant "come here" or do a certain thing immediately, her accent was strongest.

"Listen, son. Don't pester your father about his side of the family. He doesn't like to think of them not coming around because he married a German woman or that he has all these mixed children. I have some time. Let's go to the backyard, and I will answer any questions you have."

"Mom, I just wanted to know why other people in this neighborhood have uncles, aunts, and cousins and we *don't*!"

My mom never held back from us. She felt it her right as my dad's wife and the mother of his eight kids to be able to say whatever she wanted. No, our mom was not the type of woman who was controversial or contentious. Actually, Mom was most agreeable to Pops. "Eric, I thought I shared with you all that when your father and I got married, both families didn't approve."

My mom would often try and quit smoking and then go back to smoking. I would always tell her that my school informed us that smoking wasn't good for her health. Mom would look right at me with a pretty smile and say they helped calm her nerves. The older I got, I definitely saw why this German woman living on the South Side of Chicago would need something to calm her nerves.

"Eric, I hope when you get older and have a family, you will not have the same problems your father and I have, either with family or people in general," she said as she took a couple of slow and very deliberate drags from one of her Camel nonfiltered cigarettes. Mom repositioned herself in one of our metal lawn chairs that we spray-painted red. We were sitting on our patio made from those long flat stones. Mom and Pops would get the radio out and turn to a radio station playing German music—or as we called it, "Lawrence Welk" type music—and just chill. It was all right when I or my sisters were younger, but the older we got, we became embarrassed as our friends would make fun of this foreign stuff they heard bellowing from our backyard.

"Y'alls mom and nim [referring to Pops] be tripping on that Hitler music!" I never really got mad because I felt if me and my sisters didn't like the stuff, what did we expect from people on the block?

"Mom, I know why your family can't make it here to visit, but Dad's side doesn't come around because of us?"

"Eric, they have never liked your father and I being married. It isn't about you children. They don't believe in two people from two different races getting together."

"Mom, does your family not like you and Dad being married either?"

"Well, Eric, to be very honest, they don't like that I married, for one, an American soldier, and for two, a Black man. And they think I'm crazy for moving anywhere in America, not to speak of an all-Black area." My mother never referred to our neighborhood as a ghetto. I know she hated living in the projects because of people being hostile toward her there. But again, I can never recall her talking our area down. Mom would always tell us that when people are faced with a different or unfamiliar thing, they often act badly, as she would put it.

I have heard arguments throughout the years about interracial marriages, and maybe it's me, but it always seemed certain facts or truths were not given, or maybe the people on the panel that were discussing the topic didn't want to harm anyone, specially someone in their family, being considered a half-breed, mixed, mulatto, or whatever people used in describing a person or group of people that are biracial. Certain names carry a very negative vibe. I called this chapter "Outcasts" because at times, that is how I and my sisters felt.

People don't plan to fall in love, or most children aren't planned, but the parents (or in a lot of cases, the single parent) needs to be conscious that being of two races has its own problems. Most parents I have had the opportunity to speak with as I became an adult really aren't aware that their child or children are facing an identity crisis. The parent might have been picked on or ridiculed for various reasons, but chances are, their nationality or race was never called into question. I saw Derek Jeter, the famed New York Yankee ballplayer, on TV one day and said out loud to a partner of mine, "I didn't realize this dude was Black!"

Barry looked at me and said, "Hell, Eric, he looks like you did back in the eighties." I recall Barry and I having one of our philosophical conversations, which were many. We talked about how well Jeter played the game, and I felt as though no one seemed to ever mention that he was biracial, just that he was this celebrated ballplayer. I, on the other hand, had experienced discrimination daily. It's a trip when you get it from both races. White people would just look intently at us and ask what we were. Then we get around Black folks, and they would say, "Are y'all mixed or light skinned?"

I have had a variety of jobs after being honorably discharged from the US Air Force, and everywhere I have worked, people always wanted to know what nationality I was. I don't have a problem now that people are curious. Depending on how a person steps to me is whether I give them a decent answer or not. I know that may sound childish, but no one likes a person trying to clown them. I have, at various periods in my life, even as an adult, felt out of place in certain situations.

I remember this particular event as though it happened today. In actuality, it took place some time ago. I was working in Nashville, Tennessee, as an air traffic operations coordinator with Barton Air Traffic, a civilian contracting corporation. I recall being very excited about this career move I made from being an air traffic controller, located at Richards-Gebaur Airport in Missouri. We controlled a variety of military and some civilian air operations. I arrived at the headquarters of Barton ATC. I had been working for the company for about a year in Kansas City when I was told I had been considered for an operations position at the headquarters in Nashville. Mr. Travis Pearson, the company vice president, was impressed with my military record as well as the work I was doing at Richards-Gebaur. Travis Pearson made a special trip to Kansas City supposedly to inspect our operation. I could tell from our conversation that he was evaluating me. He asked me a variety of questions pertaining to air traffic operations performed at our facility and then asked some questions about me personally.

"Eric, how long have you been married? What things do you like to do when you aren't working?"

Travis Pearson had been a chief master sergeant in the Air Force, with thirty years of active duty service. Travis was about no more than fifty years old and in excellent shape. He was a very distinguished looking White man that carried a very confident demeanor. Travis always spoke very deliberately and was straightforward. If you never met this man before, you would presume this man was in charge of something. About three months had gone by, and I was enjoying my career, although my personal life was on the rocks. I put extra effort in my work as to emotionally hide from the fact that my wife, Rochelle, and I were separated. Since she had custodial care of my two children, I had far more time on my hands than I ever had since being an adult and married with kids. We did end up getting divorced! Since we have children, I see her more now than I want to! (Thanks, Rochelle, for three beautiful children.)

I arrived at work one morning in my usual early bird fashion, as I had been drilled to do in the Air Force (thanks, Sam Coney). Once I performed all the daily equipment checks and completed various reports required for the opening of this air traffic tower, I sat back and started reviewing our fac memos (facility memorandums) and other memos from our corporate office. I almost fell out of my chair after reading the following memo:

> Eric M. Smith has been selected and is being offered the operation officer position and if accepted will be required to relocate within thirty days to the corporate headquarters in Nashville, Tennessee. Detailed information will be given to the chief of the facility and to Eric himself once position has been accepted by Eric and the facility chief notifies our office.

I thought since things weren't going well for me and my wife here, this would be the perfect opportunity. It was a promotion and a chance to get away from certain family members who I thought had been interfering in our marriage. I accepted the position and relocated to Tennessee. Once I arrived at the headquarters, I wanted to make a strong impact to let them know they made a wise choice in selecting me. I always dressed in a business manner. I either wore a suit and tie or slacks, shirt, and tie. My shoes never had anything less than a military inspection shine, and my hair was maintained as if I was still in the military, cut short with a skin fade. I maintained a 35-10 (AF dress code regulation) haircut. I kept my mustache once in civilian life as I did while serving in the military. I could, at any time, had gone up before any military formation and passed their inspection with flying colors. As I stated, I wanted to stand out as one of the best workers at the headquarters.

Apparently, after a few months had gone by and Travis and other corporate officers were comfortable with me being the new kid on the job, I noticed they would make sly comments about the clothes I wore, the way I talked, my walk, and other various things they noticed about me. I called an older friend named Carl Gibson, who was a self-appointed mentor of mine. Carl was a fifty something Black supervisor with Barton Air Traffic who had retired with twenty plus years active duty service in the Air Force. Almost all the people employed by Barton ATC were prior Air Force, Army, or Navy controllers. Very few, if any, had been civilian controllers.

I told Carl of the things that had been going on within the office and asked how he would go about handling things. Carl would tell me just to concentrate on doing the best job I could do but to not take any shit from these people and never let my guard down. "Eric, do you recall me telling you that you may be this high yellow dude with good hair and speak well, but you are still as dark as I am to them." After the few talks Carl and I had, I decided to pay very little attention to the racially slurred comments made.

I continued working and occasionally attending various corporate functions. After all, I made a change. They told me from time to time that I couldn't go back to my old facility. I worked for Barton for two years and thought my performance had been more than satisfactory. After I returned from training FedEx people with their pushback operations at FedEx's hub located in Memphis, Tennessee, Travis Pearson found out through one of the other trainers that FedEx had offered me a position with the company. I was given a raise and very diabolically treated with more respect than I had in the previous months. A couple of months passed, and I was called in the corporate meeting room and given a slip of paper that read, in effect, that my services were not needed any longer, and I was to immediately vacate the premises. I was in shock as I hoped that this was some type of sick practical joke.

Of course, I asked why I was treated this way and why I had not received some type of notice. I was told the corporation was downsizing, and unfortunately, my position was the last to be created, so I was the first to go. I was never given the opportunity to go to another facility as a controller, though I still maintained a controller's license. I moved on and sought employment elsewhere. One afternoon, I received a call from one of the guys I worked with and asked if I had some time to go and have a couple of beers. I really wasn't the beer drinking type, but this invite came as such a surprise from an individual. We only shared a lunch or two the entire time I worked with him. I would realize that day that all of my suspicions held about color or race being so significant throughout the years were actually not imagined as so many people made them seem.

I arrived at the bar and grill we agreed to meet at. I scanned the eating area and didn't see Bill. As I walked toward the bar area, I heard a feeble voice call out my name. I turned and looked toward the voice, and I could see Bill sitting at a darkened corner booth.

"Bill, how are you doing?"

"The question is, Eric, how are you doing?"

I could immediately tell Bill carried himself well and was one of the few that treated me with respect! I can't ever recall him joining in the stupid remarks, so we were cool. Bill told me he had been there for about an hour before our predetermined time agreed upon.

"Bill, looks like you must be feeling pretty good."

"No, Eric, I'm really not. I have something I like to get off my chest."

"Okay, Bill, what's up?"

"Eric, some of us miss you at the office, and I felt like I had to tell you the real reason you aren't there any longer." Bill kept looking around as though he was getting ready to tell me some type of *top secret* info!

"Okay, Bill, you have my full attention."

Bill kept offering me a beer and obviously wasn't about to tell me a damn thing until I had a beer and he had another. "Hey, miss, get me another Bud and one for my friend too! Eric, I'll get straight to it. They laid you off because when they hired you, they thought they were getting a man who put down *Black* on his personal information file but would act more White because you were the lightest person and had the kind of hair you do! They said you acted too *Black*!"

I was in temporary shock! Now my suspicions were confirmed!

"I can remember, Eric, when you were hired, Travis needed to hire a *Black* person at the corporate office to show people interested that the company gave *Blacks* a chance to be in management. He often said if it were up to him, he wouldn't have promoted *Blacks* in the military, and he definitely wouldn't put any in management."

I just sat there, looking at this white dude, all red in the face from the few beers he drank to muster the strength to tell me this!

After urging him to continue, Bill told me the corporate officers were never impressed with my attendance or my neat appearance that all the other employees noticed! He said that I had been selected only because I was the lightest *Black* person they had interviewed. My military record or my work performance had nothing to do with the selection! An hour had passed, and I really didn't say much at all! Bill kept apologizing, and I told Bill I appreciated him being so honest. Bill looked as if a ton of bricks were removed from his back.

This event reminded me of the one mentioned in my chapter "Calumet," where the *Black* coach disqualified me from making the team my freshman year because of the opposite! He thought because of being a light-skinned half-breed (as opposed to a darker-skinned one), I wouldn't be tough enough to be on his team. I often wonder, how many generations will it take to do away with the *color* or *race* issue?

Maybe *half-and-half* (mixed) people won't feel like *outcasts* in the future!

17

Choosing Sides

This chapter could have been a book within itself! I don't contend to be some all-knowing guru on the biracial—in particular, White-Black—marriages, or in some cases, two people getting together intimately and producing a child! Although, I believe I have an insider's view on the subject! I'm sure some authors would love to have a disclaimer on certain things in their books. I certainly hope the information written in this chapter will not cause any problems for people. I really became aware of the necessity of a book like this when I read an article on the 2000 census report and how people had been so alarmed that officials felt as though the info received from the census needed public attention.

It is no secret that the Hispanic growth in this country had, even prior to the census taken, been considered the largest and fastest growing minority! I paid close attention to various newspaper and magazine articles as well as reports on different TV programs about the officials that tallied the numbers and facts from the census. I sat there really happy that times were changing, and people must be either more comfortable or more knowledgeable about their heritage than the last census taken in 1980.

I couldn't help but think maybe now people will not be so obsessed with the color of a person's skin or someone having to choose one nationality over another!

I don't feel like some folks want to let this racial thing go because they are getting paid and love being in the limelight from people having to choose sides. White this, Hispanic that, African American this, it all trips me out!

When I'm in church and looking around, I think of the scripture about us being created in God's image. That means us, human beings! I'm not a biblical scholar, but I can't find anything on color! I have read about slavery and the differences between nationalities, but except for the constant mention of the descendants of Israel, who are Jews, there aren't any distinctions between races or colors!

I listen to a variety of radio programs. When I want to be entertained, I turn on the Tom Joyner oldies station. People who listen to this syndicated radio program know that it not only offers songs that other radio stations haven't played in years but also gives you a variety of on the air theatrics! I listen to this program because of the oldies or the famous or maybe infamous "sky shows" that are broadcast live in cities with a large African American population. This radio program caters to Black folks' interest! Tom Joyner is not considered biracial but is no darker than I am (high yellow)! Tom has a cast of people that are undisputedly hilarious! My favorite, although he clowns yellow brothers all the time, is Jay Anthony Brown! Here you have this chubby dark-skinned comedian that would fit on any corner, making people laugh in these states that are often referred to as united (are they?). His humor is direct, and Jay lovingly and affectionately is referred to as a *fool* by some of us commenting on his comedy!

Mr. Tavis Smiley's political and philosophical comments are enjoyed by a variety of people. Tavis says things and points to certain matters that are dramatically ignored by our country's mainstream media.

Although I truly like Tavis's commentaries, I wonder how successful this brother would be if times would change and skin color and race were not so important in this country. I'm sure as educated and sharp as Tavis is, he would find some way to make a good living for himself. I have looked and listened to the *Rush Limbaugh* program, and truthfully speaking, he makes me sick with his opinions and his, at more times than not, distorted views on our country's affairs. I'm not crazy. I realize if I truly wanted to and maybe weren't raised on the South Side of Chicago and developed what White people consider a militant attitude, I could cut my hair low, have no facial hair, change my walk, speak softer, and without using my characteristic hand and body gestures, learn and play golf (sorry, Tiger, I know brothers golf too!) and a variety of other personal changes and fit in as a White boy that can dance a little (very little, my kids say) and can, in my younger days, uncharacteristically run as fast as any brother around!

I look at some young mixed kids who look like me or my sisters and talk very proper, which is still considered in the hood to sound as though they're White, and wonder if they are having a problem with having an identity. Questions run through my mind like, Is there anyone in this kid's life who can help them understand who they are? Do these children have one or both parents helping them cope with being biracial? Again, I don't have a degree in psychology from a prestigious university or have attained some outstanding accomplishment. If a psychologist offered the results of a clinical study that took thirty plus years to complete, the written conclusion would, in most cases, be highly respected and regarded as scientific fact.

I'm sure just as I have written this version of growing up biracial, there will be someone who will say that I was wrong and I only speak for myself and perhaps my own dysfunctional family. They will speak of their own child-rearing years and their family's personal experience as being normal, no type of identify problems. I won't ever call someone out of their life experiences. But having talked with other biracial (I refer primarily to Black-White product) people through the years, the overwhelming majority offers very similar experiences I have spoken of in this book.

I enjoyed a recent book *Check All That Apply* by Sundee Tucker Frasier. This particular book had to be one of the best I have read concerning biracial people. It's a required reading! Thank you, Sundee. I look forward to your next book!

I have read various writings from either psychologists or self-help authors that I most definitely agree with. Any people can escape the mental hold, but they are often "products of their environment."

I grew up hating hearing that term in school. It seemed as though many books I read used this term to tell people you can't help being like you are and forget trying to change because after all, you are a product or your environment. I have met other mixed people that took on the attitude and demeanor of the White parent. I recall this young lady in class at Kansas City, Kansas Community College. She reminded me of one of my seven sisters, particularly Lori Ann. She was high yellow, to use a term familiar to some folks. She would say hello after a few classes together, but we never really spoke until this particular evening.

I noticed there were about five or six Blacks in our class, a few Hispanic people, and the rest White, including our instructor. We happened to get on the subject of minority-owned businesses. The discussion started out normal and very light, but it soon turned into a debate that the instructor was enjoying as much as I did. All of a sudden, reparations came into discussion when one of the Black students commented on how the biggest business our country profited on was slavery. I was astonished this instructor didn't come unglued. He must have been either interested in this topic of discussion or perhaps concluded personally that the statement made by this student was true, that slavery was one of the biggest and most profitable businesses this country had. This instructor as well as my classmates might not have known that I regarded myself as Black, but they would soon find out from my very opinionated comments.

"Mr. Smith, you sure do have a very strong opinion about this reparations topic."

I assumed my instructor never guessed my age because he often talked to me as though I was one of his younger students. He was only three years older than me, although he looked like he was well into his forties. I was thirty-five and no doubt one of the older students in class.

"Yes, I agree there has been a great disadvantage, but we are making strides."

The instructor gave me a look I have seen my entire life when a person appeared to be in shock when I identified myself as a Black person. For a brief moment, without me showing any expression, a few classmates and my instructor visibly showed amazement at my racial identification. I scanned the room and saw a few people who appeared not to be surprised. They probably figured I was either a light-skinned Black or Hispanic.

I was the one knocked off my chair when the light-skinned young lady, who normally spoke with a soft voice, said, "I am biracial, and I don't believe in our government owing Black people anything." She gave me one of the most hateful looks a person could give another.

My son Eric Jr. would have said, "Pops, that chick was mean muggin' you." I thought, had this woman have been a dude, we might have been scrappin'. The discussion went on, and I sat there in amazement at this pretty woman who was in her mid-twenties. She spoke in my mind with the same mentality of a White person. After class, I hurried past other students and asked her if she had a moment. I was always groomed and dressed well, so I guess the way she hesitated when I asked her, she looked intently at me, paused, and started walking toward the wall. I immediately let her know that I had a girlfriend and was in a content relationship. Her body language showed she relaxed. She was a fine woman and probably used to men, especially brothers, hittin' (pick up) on her.

"I didn't mean to upset you in class. It's interesting how different our opinions are. I'm mixed too. My mother was German, and my father was Black."

"Well, I really wasn't upset with you. I get tired of Black people using slavery as an excuse." I was burning up inside as she kept talking. It sounded as though I was conversating with Rush Limbaugh. In the middle of her talking to me, she said, "My father is White and my mother is Black, and I went to school in Johnson County." She knew that statement would let anyone know that she probably considered herself above all the "White man holding Black people down" stuff was not true. Johnson County is considered within the five top richest counties in the Unites States. Also, the fact that her daddy was White made plenty of sense why she thought the Black struggle was only imagined.

We talked for no more than ten minutes. That ten minutes seemed like an hour. "What school did you graduate from? When did you graduate?" I told her Leavenworth High School. I was always reluctant to offer the year, not because I was vain but because I knew some people didn't believe me and would often think I was clowning around. I was told I didn't look any older than in my late twenties. It's nice to look younger than you really are, but the age thing seemed to take over the conversation, and often the topic or event being discussed were put on a back burner. She could tell by my conversation that I wasn't interested in her romantically or making her uncomfortable with any advances that this fine girl probably had grown accustomed to for years.

"I apologize for giving you such a mean look. It's just I get so tired of people always asking what I am or some people blaming White people for all their own personal failures." She asked various questions. "Did your sisters go through a lot of things? Was it hard growing up in the inner city?" After I answered a few questions she threw at me, I asked her a few myself. She had only one other brother, who she said was ten years younger than her. The questions she appeared to avoid were those about her father. I gathered from what she did say that her family was at least (*economically*) upper middle class, if not better. Her mother was some type of career professional, and her father, she related, owned a small business. She, without any hesitation, let me know that although she attained her mother's physical characteristics, she chose her father's philosophical ideology. It amazed me how different our views were. It appeared we do often choose sides by the environment we are raised in.

18

Breed

There is an old-school song by Frankie Beverly & Maze called "Joy and Pain." That song always had a special meaning to me. I related a lot of things in my life to the lyrics expressed so well by the above-mentioned artist. The song went on to say that loving a person was like having sunshine and rain, which we all know is needed to make any living thing grow. Zebra, half-breed, White boy, White nigga, colored boy, high yellow, mixed, mixed nigga, redbone, and probably a few others I have forgotten. I now laugh at the names I have mentioned, but I am also forty-two years old. I recall a few years ago I was at Kensington gym (Kansas, City, Kansas). I was thirty-five and still had enough basketball skills to walk in most gyms and be picked up for a run with no problem. After saying what's up to a few fellas, I asked who had *line* (next game). There were about twenty plus fellas (all brothers) in the gym, and I counted about four *lines* before I could call next *line*. I decided to see if I could jump on someone's team since all the *lines* couldn't have had their players already selected. This one brother named James, who I had been playing ball with for years, spoke up. "Hey, E, you can run with me."

I didn't have the quickness and jumping ability I had when we were considered real ballers, but neither did James. He knew we both might have lost a step, but we still could squeeze off a jumper that would go in or make a good pass or two. In any gym across America, if you are older than thirty years old, you are probably considered old school when you step on the court. Most of the dudes knew me and knew I might not be able to take over a game anymore or be considered as a go-to player.

I once would have been, but I played within my thirty-five-year-old ability. James and a few of us cracked on older player's abilities (gravity is a monster), or should I dare say the lack of. We also marveled at how these young cats all seemed to play above the rim. We reminisced on whatever type of game we played when we were younger.

"Man, y'all old dudes be trippin' us out about y'all being able to run us out of the gym when y'all was younger."

Some of these young dudes would come up to some of us after the run and say no louder than a whisper, "Hey, man, that was a decent move you did. I guess you must have had some skills when you were younger, huh?" They would whisper these compliments as to not to let the other younger brothers know they even acknowledged our skills. We were also being referred to as old dudes when we looked at ourselves as a little older but still ballplayers. James's _line_ had two games down from the game being played on the court.

This dude walked in the gym all geared up as to try and let everyone who might not have known him think he was a baller. James and a few others knew him, but I hadn't seen him before, and he hadn't ever seen me before now. Things are different in a gym when playing with White guys. You can wear any type of outfit and someone will pick you up whether they know you or not. In a gym with all Black dudes playing, if someone doesn't know you, you better have on some matching gear and most definitely a pair of almost new basketball shoes on or be six-three or bigger to have anyone pick you up.

"Eric, here comes this nigga that thinks he's Michael Jordan or somebody." James never really had anything bad to say about anyone, I recall thinking, but I soon found out this brother was loud and walked around talking about the game being played on the floor as if someone told him he was skilled enough as to assess someone's game.

"James, let me run wit y'all."

"Sorry, man, I got my five." He and I briefly looked at each other and nodded as to nonverbally say, "What's up?"

"Hey, man, who all you got?" He had already tried to get on a couple of *lines* ahead of James, and people already had their crew they were running with. James didn't specifically answer him. "Come on, James. Let me run." This dude knew, as the rest of us did, that if you had to wait and get a new *line*, you would be sitting for possibly a couple of hours with the amount of *lines* already established. I, being one of the older dudes at the gym, fellas knew I often broke up arguments that could and often escalate into a few fists thrown. "Come on, James. Who all running wit you?"

"Man, I already told you I got my five."

This dude was just standing to the side of the bleachers we were sitting at, dribbling a ball. I had gotten up and went to say what's up to a couple of partners, wondering how long this dude would have to wait if he couldn't get on someone's squad. Once I returned and sat back down next to James, he started to tell me about how this dude started trippin' about me running on James's squad when I heard, "How you gonna let this half-breed nigga run and not pick me up?" James and I stopped talking, and for the first time in years, I felt all swollen up and thought I knew this big head nigga was not startin' no dumb shit over playin' some ball.

I thought, *Please, Lord, let this dude go on somewhere.* After James and I paused a minute, we resumed our conversation. James was a reformed thug who, now being in his mid to late thirties, enjoyed playing a little ball when not working and trying to take care of his family, as most older dudes here at this gym were doing.

"James, come on, man. This half-breed nigga can't play no ball." This dude was talking as if I wasn't anywhere around. He was so loud that he drew the attention of the fellas playing on the court. I thought I was past the thoughts and feelings that was stirring up in my mind.

I stood up. "Yo, man, what in the hell is yo problem?" My vocabulary changed when I was near a basketball court, whether inside or out. I seemed to only use the word *nigga* when someone started trying to bully me or perhaps my team around. When I was younger, I used *nigga* in my vocabulary as often as I heard the young dudes use it today. A few times, brothers who didn't know me and wasn't sure if I was half Black or Hispanic would give me a slight look when I used that word. Normally, they assessed from my ball handling and moves on the court that I must be mixed or from possibly the way I carried myself that it was okay! I thought I was just another nigga doing whatever was going on. A few of the fellas stopped their conversations and just started looking at us. The fellas that knew me probably were wondering what in the hell this dude could have said to make me jump up and get off with this fool. I had long since stopped any type of arguing or scrapping with anyone over bad calls on the court, or for that fact, anything.

"You yellow half-breed niggas ain't got no skills on the court, and I know you can't box!"

The last time I had a fight was with my sister Inge's man a few years prior to this event. I believed I was way past fighting unless someone broke into my house or attacked someone in my family. Once I turned thirty or so, I resolved within myself that I would only fight if someone threatened me or my family's physical safety. After all, I probably logged more fights than Roberto Duran had in his boxing career, which was a considerable amount.

I guess I forgot my age and the fact that I just had a long conversation with my oldest son, Eric Jr., a few days ago when he was suspended from high school for fighting this White dude for calling him nigga. "You come up here with yo country ass beggin' somebody to let yo punk ass play. If you think I can't box, then run yo big head ass over here, *nigga*!"

Fellas throughout the gym started laughing loud and saying, "Boy, you better watch out. You done got this nigga mad."

The dude started walking toward me, and I didn't move. I just threw up my hands in a very familiar, although longed to be forgotten, way. James and a few of the older dudes got in between us and urged us to stop this. "Man, y'all know y'all old niggas need to quit this!"

"Come on, E. Don't let this dude bring out the old Eric!"

This dude just looked at James and threw his hands up. "Y'all niggas trippin'. I got last *lines.*"

I sat down for a moment then went and grabbed a ball and started dribbling as I was getting ready. Our game was next. I reached the age that I tried to resolve almost all conflicts. I played a couple of games, then this dude stepped on the court. It was his run. I very reluctantly walked slowly toward him and held my hand out to shake and just play ball. He reluctantly returned the extended hand out. We shook and played the game. I could tell this gesture was favorable to the older crowd, but I was sneered at by the younger fellas in the gym. When you're younger, *respect* is nonnegotiable in the streets. It means everything!

Being a mulatto (half Black, half White), half-breed, mixed, or whatever is nothing to be ashamed of. Parents need to teach their children the values of both heritage. Doing so will instill confidence and a positive identity within your children so they can grow up knowing who they are and able to handle ridicule without getting physical. Since I didn't grow up around White people, I didn't have events like the abovementioned one that I, throughout my youth, experienced living in an all-Black community as often concerning White people.

Any African American who doesn't mind being truthful will tell you we have always made an issue of the light-skinned and darker-skinned people within our own race. White America generally wants people to think they have grown past the color issue when truthfully speaking, they don't want their children doing much more than socializing academically or perhaps athletically with Black people. The books I have read on slavery proves that half-breeds or very light-skinned people were afforded better treatment more often than non-mixed or darker-skinned slaves. That is no doubt where this skin color resentment comes in within the Black race.

Don't feel out of place if you are a biracial person. Embrace both cultures and realize you happen to live in a country here in America that was built on different cultures and nationalities.

19

Finally

The year is 2002, and I have been blessed to reach the age of forty-two years young. The statement made years ago by my parents have proven to be one the most profound statements in my life: "Son, we pray you reach the age where you don't live your life by other people's standards or perceptions. You just enjoy *life*."

For all of my young life and well into adult life, I have tried to find out the real person. I have always been fairly confident (borderline arrogant) in my endeavors, although this identity thing always seemed to be in question. My sisters and I have had people ask us what we were for so long that a lot of us probably spent a majority of our adult lives seeking the answer to those type of questions. I know I did everything within my mental and emotional power to instill in my children and the nieces and nephews I have been in contact with a very strong sense of who they are and tried giving them a true sense of direction.

I have concluded in life that without a true sense of self-identity, people often never reach their life's potential. God has stated in his Word that all men (and women) were created in his own image. I never read that a certain color of skin made a person any better or worse than another. I recently went to Los Angeles for a weekend vacation and had the opportunity to revisit some places I had been to when I was in the Air Force and stationed in Victorville, California. I went to Venice Beach, rented a beach cruiser, and marveled just how many different nationalities were mingling on the beach and the boardwalk. I rode for two hours and truly appreciated how people just got along, even if only in a casual way. I saw so many mixed children that I thought for a moment this must be one of the most interracial cities I have been to here in the US.

In the past, as this book has indicated, I had been considered a ballplayer within the recreational level. I played in and against the nonprofessional ballers I have shared a court with. I haven't played at the nationally known Rucker Park in New York, but I can assure you there are basketball courts I have played at and ballplayers I have played with and against that skills would match a few people in the NBA. I stopped and saw, for the first time I can recall, almost as many White ballers as Black ballers on one court at the same time. I rode on and watched the skater's area and again looked on as there appeared to be no issue of color. Blacks were skating and talking to Whites. I realize we look at a person and assume that they are an African American or European American simply by their skin tone, but listening to some people speak with accents or other languages when I was sure they were a White or Black American confirmed what I have always known—that often people are placed in a nationality category by skin color and absolutely no other physical characteristic. It seems to be the norm!

I don't want to sound like Gandhi. I realize there are problems here in the US that are more severe than discrimination against someone because of color or race, but almost everything we see on TV or read about in newspapers seem to gravitate toward race issues.

The following statement is strictly my own opinion and doesn't reflect those of my other family members or friends. *Everyone* has some type of prejudice toward another person or group of people. These are simply likes and dislikes of certain things a person or a group of people do in their actions that someone doesn't like. I recall having a friend that didn't like men that were a lot shorter than he was. I knew someone who didn't like people with accents. We are all are part of the *human race*. We are God's creation. How long will it take for people to see that color or race doesn't matter much at all?

This statement will probably cause several people to trip. I strongly believe in the *reparations* bill that our Congress will continue to ignore as long as possible and, when they have to, fight this issue to the death. With that statement said and everyone agreeing that our country participated in one of the worst atrocities the world has unfortunately inflicted upon any race of people, we can move past this issue only after the wrongs have openly been acknowledged.

A White person can't address certain things about Hispanics and especially about Black people that irritate the hell out of them because if done so publicly, they would be forever branded a *racist*. A Black person can basically say anything about another group of people, and it is far more tolerated. *Why?* Jesse Jackson can openly accuse a White politician of allowing crime and economic problems to go unnoticed in our urban cities without he himself being called anything other than a concerned American. When that same politician fires back and states that we need more Black churches and families to be involved with our own communities, he is perhaps called a racist and has probably cut his political throat.

My father told me there were times growing up in the South that a Black couldn't laugh out loud. Also, in some areas as recent as the 1960s, a Black person had to step aside or off the sidewalk to let a White person pass by. I loved hearing my parents, who rarely talked about the differences between the races, sit down and actually bring up things that are obvious and some not so obvious.

If the US would simply put together some type of holiday to recognize an open *apology* for slavery in this country and the long-lasting effects it has had from one generation to another since the Emancipation Proclamation, and in addition put together some type of reparations package (money, credit repair, something), race relations would become better overnight. People need not forget that the civil rights struggle was not a hundred years ago but a mere forty plus years. Only two generations passed when Black people were openly discriminated against, even by our own country's laws and practices.

Martin Luther King Jr's speech "I Have a Dream" has always touched me. I was nine years old when Reverend King was assassinated. I have always enjoyed reading about Martin and Malcolm X. I truly believe there were forces that knew that if these two men would ever come together with their philosophies and ideologies, millions of people, Blacks and Whites, would have put the race issues aside and treated all men and woman, no matter the color, better.

Working on this book for the past few years has made me more observant than I had been in the past, and as I look at various television programs and news articles, I realize we haven't come very far within the past three or four decades. Oh, I'm sure some folks might downplay the color issue and try to pretend this race issue in our country has made some major progress. Has it?

Look at our prisons across this nation. Look at the urban setting and the things allowed within the inner cities and how tight and fast law enforcement reacts to problems in our suburbs. Large companies and corporations have diversification training. Why can't we as a country (*government*) be honest that race and color issues are as big a problem as they have ever been? I contend that there are major differences between Black and White people, from the way we worship, how we raise our children, to why for the average White person starting a college fund appears to be more important than a child always wearing the latest and most up-to-date apparel that we as Blacks pride ourselves in. Even in our current times, a White man may go in for a job with a beard and long hair, and his credentials are evaluated more than his appearance. A Black man goes in for the same job, and he had better be neatly shaven, haircut sculptured to his head, and have a very neat appearance or his credentials might not even be looked at. This type of thing does go on.

African Americans only comprise approximately 14 to 15 percent of our nation's population. So a person of another country might ask why there is such a race issue with Black people having such a small percentage of the United States population. Simple. Every US citizen knows how unequal Black people have been treated in this country. Also, there is the fact that our great country was built on free labor (*slavery*). I say again, if Congress would simply acknowledge publicly that slavery was wrong and the terrible ramifications passed on generations long after slavery ended, things would change immediately. If certain things in this book are offensive, it wasn't meant to be!

I hated this biracial status for a good majority of my life. And then one day, I started looking at myself differently. I attribute this directly to prayer. I reached a low in my life about certain situations I found myself in and turned to God for answers. Jesus told us that if we keep asking, we shall receive. I thank God. He has allowed the completion of this book to weigh on my mind until I completed it. I only pray it helps someone to realize that they are a child of God, and they, too, were put here for a reason. Pursue your dreams!

My sisters and I have always been truly in the middle, and I recall them, maybe more than I, ridiculed and evaluated simply because they were a little darker than some White people and much lighter than Black people. Please take the time with your children and tell them how special they are and that color or race doesn't make you any better or worse than the next person.

I called this chapter "Finally" because I feel that I finally see that this biracial status that I ran from and at times even hid from emotionally has been truly a blessing in disguise. I now know that all the time I wondered why I felt certain ways and did things different than some friends were because we were born from parents who were different in color and nationality, as well as culturally. I pray my sisters are able to attain this feeling of contentment and reach a positive feeling for themselves!

The next time you are sitting at work, using public transportation, in a park or anywhere, look over at someone briefly and try and look past their physical features or that he or she is White, Black, light, or dark and see that person is not any different than you are. (Don't just stare. Some folks are crazy.)

There are, without any doubt, major differences between races, whether it is physical or just how a group of people do things. We are all trying to live and take care of ourselves and our families. If you happen to be a biracial person, don't feel as though you must choose sides. Enjoy the things each race has to offer. Be *proud*!

About the Author

Eric Smith and his seven sisters are classified as African German American, their mother being from Berlin, Germany, and their father being from the United states. He was born in 1960 at 929 N. Hudson Streeet, on the ninth floor of the Cabrini-Green housing projects, Chicago, Illinois. Their family moved to Eighty-Second and Emerald (South Side Chicago). He attended Calumet High School his freshman and sophomore year. They relocated in 1976 to Leavenworth, Kansas.

Eric graduated Leavenworth High class of 1978. This is a story that plainly describes being, at that time, a minority, biracial, or mixed within the minority (African American). He and his sisters are fair skinned or high yellow. From grade school to present (2021), he was asked what nationality he was. Wow, still in 2021! He strongly believes his book will answer most questions people have about interracial marriage that produce biracial children from a person who lived it. When he was much younger, he felt like he was fully dressed in a football uniform, standing center court in a basketball arena, and *everyone* looked at him, wondering who or what the hell this guy was doing! Race and a person's color are still issues in 2021.

CPSIA information can be obtained
at www.ICGtesting.com
Printed in the USA
BVHW071512011121
620453BV00006B/275

9 781662 444623